How to Start, Run & Grow a Residential and Commercial Cleaning Business

BY

Maria Carmen

Copyright © 2016 - CSB Academy Publishing Company
All Rights Reserved.

No part of this publication may be reproduced, stored in a retrieval system, or transmitted in any form or by any means, electronic, mechanical, photocopying, recording, or otherwise without the proper written consent of the copyright holder, except brief quotations used in a review.
Published by:

CSB Academy Publishing

CSB Academy Publishing Company

Cover & Interior designed

By

David Miller

First Edition

Table of Contents

About Me 15
Introduction... 18
    In-Demand Services 18
    Start on a Budget.................................. 18
    Franchise or Independent Business? 19
        Instant Business 20
        Brand Awareness 20
        Marketing and Promotion 20
        Training and Support 21
        Cost 21
        Control 22
        Site Location 22
        Resale Value / Profit Sharing.................. 22
    Do You Have What It Takes?..................... 23
The Basics of Cleaning Business 25
    What is Residential Cleaning 25
    What is Commercial Cleaning.................... 25
    Work Environment................................. 26
    Skills and Competencies.......................... 27
Income Potential 28
    Earning Potential for Residential Cleaning 28
    Earning Potential for Commercial Cleaning... 29
    Specialized Cleaning and Earning Potential .. 30
        Restoration 31

Trauma and Crime Scene Cleaning 31
Repair Services 31
Specialized Floor Care 32
High Tech and Bio-Tech Firm 32
Food Processing Sites 32
Expert Witness 32
Education, Training, and Consulting 33

12 Steps to Start a Residential Cleaning Business 34

Business Plan Creation 34
Naming Your Company 35
Set Up a Business Entity 35
Determine Your Target Market 36
Determine Your Rates 36
Open a Bank Account for Your Business 37
Obtain Licenses and Permits 37
Get Insurance Coverage 37
Hire an Accountant or CPA 38
Talk with an Attorney 38
Get the Necessary Business Forms 38
Market and Promote Your New Business 39

Is Residential Cleaning Right For You? 40

10 Steps to Start a Commercial Cleaning Business 41

Develop a Business Plan 41
Come Up with a Business Name 42

Determine Your Target Market 42
Setting Your Rates 43
Open a Business Bank Account.................. 44
Obtain Licenses and Permits 44
Determine What Insurance You Need 44
Be Prepared for Taxes.............................. 45
Be Prepared for Legal Issues..................... 45
Marketing & Promoting Your New Business .. 46
Is Commercial Cleaning Business Right for You? 47
What You Need to Get Started 47
Cleaning Equipment You Will Need.............. 49
Choosing the Right Vehicle 50
What to Look for When Buying a Vehicle .. 50
Safety Issues to Consider...................... 50
Other Things to Consider...................... 51
After Your Purchase 52
11 Steps for Choosing Cleaning Products and Equipment 53
1. Look for an SDS - Safety Data Sheet....... 53
2. Does It Work?................................... 54
3. How Time Efficient Is the Product 55
4. Support of Business and Safety Philosophies 56
5. You Get What You Pay For 56
6. Where to Purchase 57

7. Evaluating Cleaning Equipment 57

8. Warranty 57

9. Supply and Maintenance Costs 58

10. Cost Through the Warranty Period Compared with the Cost of Others 58

11. Expected Life of the Equipment 58

5 Types of Cleaners 59

    Neutral Cleaner 59

    All-Purpose Cleaner 60

    Glass Cleaner 60

    Acid Cleaner 60

    Degreasers 61

Choosing the Best Vacuum 61

Mop Buckets and Wringers 62

Choosing the Right Dusting Tools 64

Where to Buy Cleaning Supplies 67

    Retail Stores 67

    Wholesale Clubs 68

    Online Stores 68

    Why Buy from Janitorial Distributors 69

Legal Requirements 71

    Registering a Cleaning Business 71

    Business Structure 72

    Sole Proprietor 72

    Partnership 72

Corporation (Inc. or Ltd.) 73
S Corporation 73
Limited Liability Company (LLC) 73
Do You Need to Become Bonded? 74
Do I Need a Business License? 75
How to Become Licensed and Bonded 75
Should You Get Insurance? 76
What is CIMS? 77
Why Get Certified? 77
   What It Includes 77
Benefits of CIMS Certification 79
Establishing a Residential Cleaning Rate Structure 80
   How to Charge 81
Establish a Commercial Cleaning Rate Structure 83
   The Supply and Demand Theory 83
   Competitive Pricing 84
   Contracts and One-Time Jobs 84
      Pricing 84
How to Bid and Win Contracts 86
   10 Tips for Better Bidding 86
      1. Listen to the Customer 86
      2. Read the Contract, Specifications, and Request for Proposals 87
      3. Walk the Property 87

4. Cut Costs, Improve Quality and Share the Savings 88

5. Innovative Approaches 90

6. Respond to the Specifications and Contract; Offer Additional Options 90

7. Triple Check Bid Calculations 91

8. Realistic Expectation of Job Ability 91

9. Sell Quality Service at a Fair Price 92

10. Reinvest 92

How to Write a Commercial Job Proposal 93

6 Factors to Include in a Commercial Contract 95

7 Contract Terms and Clauses You Should Know 96

30 Days Cancellation 97

Start and End Date 97

Cost of Basic Supplies 98

Late Payment Penalty 98

Key Loss 98

Defect Deduction 98

Labor Hours Requirement 99

How to Get Your First Clients 100

How to Get Your First Residential Cleaning Clients 100

How to Get Your First Commercial Contracts 101

Networking 101

Direct Mail 101
Via Real Estate Agents 102
Display Ads in Newspapers 102
Property Management Companies 103
Phone Books 103
Websites 103
Telemarketing 104
Craigslist 104
6 Quickest Ways to Get Cleaning Jobs 105
Community Networking 105
Direct Mail Fliers 105
Real Estate Agents and Property Managers 106
Newspaper Ads 106
Websites 106
Referrals and Word of Mouth 106
How to Make Your Cleaning Company Stand Out 108
A Day in the Life inside the Cleaning Business 110
Dusting 110
Bathrooms 110
Kitchen 111
Property 111
Specialty Services 111
Commercial Cleaning 112

Safety on the Job 112
Top 10 Concerns for You and Your Employees 114
    1. Blood Borne Pathogens 114
    2. Ergonomics 114
    3. Hazardous Equipment 115
    4. Specialty Cleaning 115
    5. Professionalism 116
    6. Lead Paint 116
    7. Asbestos 117
    8. Integrated Pest Management 117
    9. Hazardous Chemicals 117
    10. Sick Building Syndrome 117

How to Effectively Run & Grow Your Cleaning Business 119
13 Ways to Make Your Cleaning Business a Success 120
    1. Always Learn New Things 120
    2. Use Your Resources 120
    3. Treat It Like Your Own Home 121
    4. Have a System 121
    5. Use Caution 121
    6. Don't Undersell 121
    7. Take Care of Employees 121
    8. Create a Niche 122
    9. Focus on Computer Skills 122

10. Keep Track of Labor Costs 122
11. Focus on Customer Service 123
12. Watch the Economy 123
13. Be Selective 123
4 Creative Ways to Win Major Accounts 124
   Know Your Target Market 124
   Fulfill a Need.. 124
   Have Initiative 125
   Be Properly Equipped 125
Top 10 Tips to Close the Sale 125
How to Hire and Train the Right Employees . 128
   What is Effective Training 128
   Why Train 129
   Identifying Core Training Needs................ 129
   Training Methodology............................ 130
   Interactive Learning............................. 132
   What Goes Into Interactive Learning 133
   Goals of Interactive Training 133
   Making It Stick..................................... 134
   Maintain Perspective 135
   Top 10 Training Tips 135
   Promoting from Within: Worker to Supervisor 136
   Developing a Pre-Lead Training Program ... 140
Monitoring Your Business and Dealing with Issues 141

What Customers Want 141

Warning Signs of Difficult Clients 142

Top Cleaning Complaints 144

5 Ways to Solve Common Cleaning Complaints 145

    Dusting 145

    Restrooms/Bathrooms 146

    Vacuuming 146

    Trash 147

    Supply Shortage 147

How to Effectively Deal with Difficult Clients 148

5 Ways to Getting Out of a Bad Contract ... 151

    Deal with It 151

    Ask for More 152

    Talk It Out 152

    Adjust the Work 152

    Walk Away 153

4 Step Analysis to Identify Future Job Contracts 153

    Watch Your Numbers 153

    Compare 153

    Risks 154

    Track Everything 154

Quality Assurance Audits 154

    Why Audit? 155

What and Where to Audit......................156

When to Audit......................................156

Who Is Auditing 157

How to Audit......................................158

Conclusion 160

11 Core Benefits of Owning Your Business .161

Potential for Unlimited Income 161

Quick Revenue 161

Start on a Budget 161

Be Your Own Boss 161

Determine Your Own Hours...................162

Daily Paychecks 162

Easy Work that Isn't Technical or Complicated 162

No Mental or Emotional Exhaustion 162

Choosing Who You Work With 163

Work from Home.................................163

Start Additional Cleaning Services..........163

SAMPLE CLEANING SERVICES AGREEMENT .165

Sample LLC/S Operating Agreement...........174

Sample Business Plan.............................195

1.0 Executive Summary 195

Introduction..195

The Company 195

Services 195

The Market 196
Financial Results 196
Chart: Highlights 196
2.0 Company Summary 198
3.0 Services 201
4.0 Market Analysis Summary 201
5.0 Strategy and Implementation Summary 205
6.0 Management Summary 217
7.0 Financial Plan 219
1 Start-up Funding 220
EMPLOYEE WRITTEN WARNING LETTER 234

About Me

Hello, my name is Maria, and I have something important to tell you.

I know you've probably heard these types of success stories before and are a little skeptical, but I'm telling you this is true and can really happen for you.

Ten years ago, after my divorce, I needed to find a way to support myself. I was one of those individuals that never went to college or had a trade skill, so there weren't a lot of job choices for me.

What was I to do? I started looking into entry-level jobs that didn't require specialized training or skills. Unfortunately, I wasn't keen on the idea of working at a fast-food restaurant for minimum wage with limited potential for advancement or better pay.

Then, I learned about house cleaning from a friend of mine. She used house cleaning as a way to supplement their family income. However, I realized the potential to grow this into something more.

So, I started taking on a few residential cleaning jobs, getting my name out there, and increasing my client list.

I took the time to do some research and found a way to offer some specialized services that got me paid a little extra. Before I knew it, my client list was growing beyond what I could do by myself. So I started hiring employees.

Then, I realized the importance of branching out and started to take on commercial contracts. Commercial cleaning turned out to be even more beneficial to my income than residential cleaning.

Not only was I able to support myself with this work, but I was able to grow and thrive. Today, I have a company of my own with 22 employees. We take on both residential and commercial cleaning contracts.

My income has grown to over $250,000 a year now. I never dreamed a simple job to help pay the bills would grow into this, but it has.

It takes a little bit of work, but the benefits are there to be had if you know what to do. I'm here to tell you what you need to do so you can have success, just like I did.

Lastly, allow me to make a quick apology in advance for any mistakes, typos, or grammatical errors you may find. As I mentioned, I never went to college, so I am not, what you might call a "well-educated nerd," but what I am is a small business owner with a passion for success.

I initially started writing this book last year, but then had to put it on the back burner for a while. Just recently, I decided to spend some time to finish what I started.

Just know that the knowledge I shared here all came from my ten years of experience in this industry.

If you like my work, I would love to see a review from you wherever you purchased this book. It would mean the world to me!

Thank you so much!

Introduction

As you probably gained from reading about me, there are two primary market groups in the cleaning industry: residential and commercial.

I'll discuss a little more about what each of these groups are a little later on in the book, but it is best if you choose a specific market to start and then expand your business as you are able.

In-Demand Services

When you choose to go into any form of cleaning, you are going into an in-demand field. According to studies, nearly half of American households are two-wage-earner households. That number is nearly 76%.

Then nearly 15% of American households are single-parent households. These facts show that a good number of American households are busy. The upside to this is that a lot of individuals choose to hire cleaning individuals since they don't have time to manage it themselves.

Start on a Budget

Perhaps another upside to starting a cleaning business is the fact that you can build a profitable business that generates revenue quickly without having to start with a lot of money. You have the flexibility to choose between a full-time or part-time business from your home or from a commercial location. To get started, you really only need a few supplies: vacuum, broom, duster, and some cleaning supplies. Then, you can get a few clients, grow your business, and add on as you need.

Franchise or Independent Business?

While one of the biggest benefits of starting a cleaning business is to build a company that meets your individual style, the main question to ask yourself before you start is whether you want to buy a franchise or start an independent business. If you have the health and time to do the work yourself, you may want to stay small and work your way up as I did.

However, for those that have more administrative skills, adequate funding, and prefer to manage others who do the work, then perhaps you would be better suited for a franchise. There are plenty of cleaning businesses out there that offer franchise opportunities.

This gives you the opportunity to work with an established name to get yourself running. It does mean you won't have as much freedom in the direction your business goes.

A franchise will work closely with you as you start your business, but you will still be responsible for keeping it running smoothly and ensuring it is profitable.

A franchise is a good option for those who don't want to gamble on starting their own system. With a franchise, you have the support of national advertising and name recognition, something that is often difficult for an individual starting their own business.

The freedom to start your own business is both an advantage and a disadvantage. It provides you the freedom to do things your way and spread into more specialized markets. However, you also have no guidelines or groundwork for relying on when you get started. Everything you learn is going to be through trial and error.

When I choose to go at it alone, I had to do a lot of research, so I could make the right decisions and start strong without making too many mistakes. Once I knew I wanted to start out on my own, the other thing I needed to ask myself was if I had what it takes.

Let's look at each area individually to help you see which option is right for you.

Instant Business

Buying into a franchise is like having an instant business. Most of the initial work is already done for you. You simply need to follow a few steps, and the business will be up and running quickly.

Brand Awareness

Perhaps the biggest benefit of buying into a franchise is the instant brand awareness. Especially if you are going with a bigger and well-known company. This means you won't have to work as hard at selling customers on your brand as you would if you were starting your own company.

Marketing and Promotion

This is similar to brand awareness. If you buy into a big name franchise, they will often assist you with marketing. Some of the larger companies even promote through national advertising campaigns. This will bring in customers to local businesses without you having to do much work at all.

Training and Support

Franchises also offer a wide range of training and support. Training is often one of the biggest reasons people choose to go with a franchise rather than a self-employed business. Before you get your company up and running, the franchise will offer some initial training and then provide you with ongoing support and even help with employees as you expand your business.

These are just a few of the benefits you can get from going with a franchise. However, this doesn't necessarily mean you should go out and find a franchise to join.

Carefully consider some of the drawbacks as well to make sure you can handle going with a franchise.

Cost

Perhaps the biggest disadvantage to a franchise is the cost. Most of the time, you have to come up with an initial down payment in order to buy into the franchise.

Some companies may also require ongoing royalty fees for the use of the company name and branding. Often these fees are a percentage (around 7%-10%) of the revenue or sales performance.

Control

If you own your own company, you are able to control a lot of the aspects of the business. On the other hand, when you buy into a franchise, you usually sign an agreement that you are following rules and operating the business in a manner already determined by the franchise.

This means you need to operate according to a set system and use specific equipment. This can be a bit constricting for some.

Site Location

This isn't as common but still happens with some franchises. One of the benefits of starting a cleaning business is the ability to operate out of your own home. With some franchises, you may be required to operate from a retail location, taking away this benefit. Some franchises even dictate where your retail location is going to be.

Resale Value / Profit Sharing

This can be another difficult one to assess. If you foresee yourself selling your business anytime in the future, this can be a bit harder with a franchise. Often a franchise won't buy you out unless the location is unprofitable, and this is the last resort.

So whether you choose to go with a franchise or not, it won't take long to get your cleaning business up and running.

Let's take a moment to see if you have what it takes. Then, we can get into discussing the process of starting your business.

Do You Have What It Takes?

Of course, the qualifications for a cleaning business will depend entirely on what type of cleaning service you want to start.

However, as with any new business owner, you are going to need a lot of dedication and determination in order to build your business from the ground up and make it successful.

Another important aspect is honesty. A client won't allow you into their home if they don't have complete trust in you.

Whether you are simply going in to clean the carpets or go into a home once a week for a thorough cleaning, people need to trust whom they are letting into their homes.

Skills-wise, there isn't much you need. I'll discuss individual skills later, but from a cleaning standpoint, you don't need much.

Knowing what cleaning solutions to use is a small portion of the skills needed for this job. Unless you plan to specialize in specific areas or a niche market that requires knowledge and a unique skill set of using special types of machines or chemicals, you really only need to know how to clean. Who hasn't done this in their own home?

Few businesses offer such a range of possibilities as cleaning. The need for general and specialized cleaning means there is a lot of increase in the future for those who choose to start a cleaning business.

So if you have what it takes, and you want to start your own business and develop financial freedom, then take the time to read this book.

In this book, I'm going to take just a brief moment to tell you about the cleaning business, in general, to help you see what you can expect. I'll also give you some information on how much you can potentially earn from this career and the specialized options you can choose to expand into.

However, the bulk of this book is going to help you get your business started. I'm going to cover the individual steps needed to start both a residential and commercial business. Since both types of businesses are fairly similar, I'll cover the main areas of supplies needed, legal requirements, how and what to charge clients, how to get contracts, making your business stand out from the others, growing your business and successfully running your new company through marketing and employee hiring and training. I'll even take the time to go over some of the major issues I've discovered in this business and how you can avoid them.

The Basics of Cleaning Business

What is Residential Cleaning

Residential cleaning is primarily made up of house cleaning services. This involves cleaning houses, apartments, condos, or vacation homes. In some cases, it can also be expanded to include any maid services done on a less frequent basis such as carpet cleaning, window cleaning, and other specialized services.

When it comes to house cleaning, you will be cleaning a home from top to bottom; but this doesn't mean that everything is included in the basics. Most residential cleaners will offer the basics such as dusting, bathroom cleaning, floor cleaning, cleaning fixtures such as appliances, mirrors, pictures, etc.

However, residential cleaning does not include cleaning clutter, bodily waste, refrigerators, stoves, ovens, moving furniture, or windows. Often these areas can be included, but an extra fee is charged.

What is Commercial Cleaning

Commercial cleaning or janitorial services often have a wider range of services than residential cleaning. Commercial cleaning can be contracted by individuals, businesses, or corporations for a variety of premises.

Some of these can include the following:

- Shops
- High Rises
- Data Centers

- Restaurants
- Offices
- Showrooms
- Warehouses
- Factories
- Schools
- Medical Facilities
- Government Facilities

While you will likely want to pick just one of these areas to start with, you can easily serve both markets at the same time once you expand your business.

Some extra services you may choose to offer through either a residential or commercial cleaning business can include the following:

- Move-in/move out cleaning
- First-time cleaning
- Extra interior cleaning
- Floorcare services
- Renovation cleaning
- Exterior cleaning
- Parking lot cleanup

The possibilities for extras that you can choose to add to your services are endless. Often after cleaning a specific building for a while, you may get a good sense of some areas that you can specialize and add on to your services.

Work Environment

Cleaning is a physically demanding job that requires you to walk, stand, climb, bend, and kneel in order to clean. You will also be pushing, pulling, lifting, and moving objects, including a twenty-pound vacuum. Repetitive arm movements, as well as repetitive bending and lifting, are required.

Whether you do the residential or commercial cleaning, you will have to be prepared to travel to and from your cleaning locations. Depending on your business, you may be required to wear uniforms or specialized outfits for protection.

Skills and Competencies

Excellent verbal and written communication skills are needed to follow job and safety instructions. You need to be detail-oriented in order to have an awareness of health and safety. Math skills may be needed in order to measure out cleaning fluids.

You should be both a team player and a self-starter. If you are working as a cleaning team, you will need to work with a team and depend on each other to get the work done. However, you may also need to work alone without supervision.

It goes without saying that physical fitness is necessary. Customer service skills, such as being friendly and professional, are needed when dealing with customers or while on-site cleaning if you are in a public area. Since you will also be around people's personal property, you will need to be trustworthy and reliable.

Lastly, you will need to have good reasoning ability to deal with any practical problems that come up while cleaning. This is also linked with a desire to learn, seek new challenges, and take on additional responsibilities.

Income Potential

Earning Potential for Residential Cleaning

For residential cleaning, you can expect an average of $10 to $25 an hour, depending on the going rates in your area. Some also choose to charge by the job, and this can be $80, $100, or $120 depending on your area and the amount of work you do.

It is up to the individual how they want to set up their cost system. Sometimes, if you are only doing one or two cleaning projects, it can be better to charge by the job, but if you are going to be doing a complete house cleaning, you may want to charge by the hour.

Let's take a quick look at how your profits would be if you charged by the job:

Number of Cleanings Per Day	Project Revenue at $80/Job	Projected Revenue at $100/Job	Projected Revenue at $150/Job
2	40,000	50,000	60,000
4	80,000	100,000	120,000
6	120,000	150,000	180,000
8	160,000	200,000	240,000
10	200,000	250,000	300,000
12	240,000	300,000	360,000
14	280,000	350,000	420,000
16	320,000	400,000	480,000
18	360,000	450,000	540,000

| 20 | 400,000 | 500,000 | 600,000 |

From this table, it easy to see how you can makeover 40,000 a year, just starting out by yourself. It isn't that hard to do two cleaning jobs a day yourself. Depending on your strength and energy, you may even be able to do four or six jobs a day yourself. On the other hand, you certainly wouldn't be able to do 20 jobs a day yourself.

This is where expanding your company and hiring employees is important. If your employees are doing two jobs a day, ten employees would easily bring your company revenue of 400,000 to 600,000 per year. We'll discuss more about employees later and how you can grow your company to this high level of revenue potential.

It should also be noted that all of these figures are based on a regular residential cleaning job. There is also the potential for add-on sales such as spring cleaning, appliance cleaning, window washing, and other specialized jobs that we covered briefly earlier.

Earning Potential for Commercial Cleaning

When it comes to commercial cleaning, the potential revenue is much greater. This is because commercial cleaning often involves a larger building and occasionally more responsibilities.

The charge per hour for commercial cleaning is an additional $5 to $15 per hour or double the cost of residential cleaning: $160, $200, $300. Of course, this would be dependent on the individual job and what is required of you.

There are going to be smaller office buildings that may not even be the size of a house, and you obviously wouldn't charge them $160. However, the following chart can also you the potential revenue for a commercial cleaning business:

Number of Cleanings Per Day	Projected Revenue at $160/Job	Projected Revenue at $200/Job	Projected Revenue at $300/Job
2	80,000	100,000	120,000
4	160,000	200,000	240,000
6	240,000	300,000	360,000
8	320,000	400,000	480,000
10	400,000	500,000	600,000

It is easy to see how quickly the revenue can add up with commercial cleaning compared to residential cleaning. However, keep in mind that since commercial cleaning is often more involved, you may not be able to do as many buildings in a day, even with additional employees.

Specialized Cleaning and Earning Potential

If you want the best of both areas, consider specialized cleaning. You will get smaller jobs like residential cleaning, but you'll get a higher pay rate like commercial cleaning.

Sometimes all you need for specialized cleaning is a team of two. Consider some specialized areas where you can make extra money with your cleaning business.

Restoration

This can include fire, water, smoke, and odor restoration. Since these types of cleaning jobs often include insurance companies and occasionally government bids, the cost and profit are going to increase. Depending on the project, most cleaning companies will charge two to ten times the typical charge.

Trauma and Crime Scene Cleaning

Most individuals don't want to do this type of cleaning, and it can be a gross job prospect. Plus, you have to be mindful of the hazardous issues of possible exposure to bodily fluids.

You often will need special training for this type of cleaning, but that can also mean you charge more.

There isn't a set cost since it will depend on what you are cleaning and how big the job is. Plus, sometimes, you will simply clean up the site, and then the insurance company or government will pay the bill you send them.

Repair Services

While not exactly cleaning, it can be another service to offer to clients, depending on your skills. Offer to repair items such as stone, tile, and wood floors. You can also repair furniture, cabinetry, and walls.

You can upholster furniture or repair leather. There are many possibilities, and you can charge based on the size and scope of the project.

Specialized Floor Care

For this, you will need special training, equipment, and chemicals so you can easily ask for a higher rate. The charge is often about $2.00 to $30.00 per square foot, depending on the surface you are cleaning and the size of the job.

High Tech and Bio-Tech Firm

Cleaning computer rooms, clean rooms, and controlled access areas are often charged at a premium rate and make even require special contracts. Often special training and materials are needed along with specific clothing and procedures. These rates are often $35.00 to $45.00 an hour.

Food Processing Sites

Anytime you are cleaning around a location responsible for food production, there are going to be specific laws, regulations, inspections, and government contracts involved. These cleaning areas are often charged an extra $5.00 to $10.00 per hour.

Expert Witness

This kind of comes along with the crime scene and trauma cleaning. Once you have established yourself as an expert, you may be used as a witness in legal cases.

However, you can also become an expert on cleaning in general and testify at trials involving injuries, cleaning procedures, mold remediation, etc. In this area, you are often paid a retainer around $2,000 to $5,000 plus an hourly rate of $250-$350. If you end up testifying in court, you may also be paid room, board, and travel.

Education, Training, and Consulting

As you can tell from the specialized areas on this list, there is also a need for people experienced in specific cleaning areas. You can then take on the job of training others who need to learn these specialized markets. The rate for this is often $25.00-$250 per hour, depending on what you are teaching and how involved the teaching process.

12 Steps to Start a Residential Cleaning Business

As I stated before, one of the main benefits of starting a residential cleaning business is the fact that you don't need a huge amount of funds to get started.

Another great benefit is you don't need a lot of special training or experience; in fact, most of your experience comes from trial and error cleaning your own home.

Residential cleaning is also an excellent part-time job to supplement your current income while you work on building and expanding your cleaning business into your only source of income.

However, there are still a few things you need to do in order to start your own cleaning business. As with any new business venture, there is some work involved before you can start getting high-profit margins.

Let's take a look at the twelve steps involved in starting a residential cleaning business.

Business Plan Creation

The business plan is the most essential part of a business' success. The document will not only provide an overall summary of your business but will also provide a detailed plan of how you will start your company and grow it. In a business plan, you need to describe how you will acquire clients, such as how you will market and promote your company.

You will also need to state how much you will charge and the specific services you plan to provide. Financial information needs to be detailed, including income statement and cash flow information. Financial data is especially important since banks or lenders will need to review it in case you need to apply for any business funding or loan. (I included a sample Business Plan at the end of the book)

Naming Your Company

It is also important to give your company a name. While you may be starting out just to make some extra money, if you truly plan to turn it into a business someday, then you need to give it a name.

You want to be creative with your name, yet simple. The name should be catchy, resonating, and memorable for customers. However, before settling on a name, make sure it isn't already being used by a company in your area or used by a national business.

Set Up a Business Entity

While a lot of business owners choose to remain sole proprietors, others choose to set up a corporation or a Limited Liability Company (LLC).

When you choose to set up a corporation or an LLC that are a number of tax and legal protections that you can take advantage of that you wouldn't otherwise have access to as a sole proprietor. You should consult with a tax or legal professional about the benefits of different types of business entities and which will be best for you.

Determine Your Target Market

It is also important that you determine who your target market is going to be early on in the business making process. Even though you are starting a residential cleaning business, you still need to provide more of a focus on your target market. You may choose to focus on a specific geographic area or neighborhood. Another option is to focus on a specific type of home, such as a condo.

Determine Your Rates

Your rates are extremely important since they have a direct impact on your company's profitability. There are several factors that will influence what you are going to charge customers. The two biggest factors are going to be your expenses and your time.

Expenses would include things such as supplies, gas, and maintenance. Other factors to include are the costs of things such as licenses and insurance.

Most residential cleaning companies choose to charge by the hour. This means you will need to develop an estimate of how much it will cost you to complete jobs based on room size, type of floors, and other cleaning needs.

One option is to contact other residential cleaning companies in your area and obtain an estimate for their rates. You will likely find that most companies have rates within a certain price range. You want to keep your rates within this range, so you don't overcharge the customer or undercut yourself.

Open a Bank Account for Your Business

Before you open your residential cleaning business, you want to start a separate bank account for your business. You can't have personal and business funds within the same account. Most banks and credit unions have special checking accounts designed specifically for small businesses.

These accounts often have a specific number of checks you can use, a debit card, and even sometimes a credit card. Be sure to discuss minimum balance requirements or maximum monthly usage fees with the financial institution before you open the account.

Obtain Licenses and Permits

Most jurisdictions are going to need you to get a license and permit to do business with the public. For a cleaning business, you often need a vendor's license. Your country clerk or county administration office can provide you with an application for this license. This type of license allows you to collect sales tax from customers. We'll cover this more in-depth later.

Get Insurance Coverage

It is also important that you apply for any insurance coverage you need. Liability insurance coverage is important in case you are injured in a customer's home or in case something is broken. You may also need to become bonded. Talk to a property and casualty insurance agent about the type of coverage you need and how much it will cost. We'll talk more about this later.

Hire an Accountant or CPA

The moment you open your residential cleaning business and start earning income, you will need to start filing business tax returns. Unless you are comfortable doing this on your own, you may want to work with an accountant or a CPA. You should also have a tax professional available that you can call on to ask tax and financial related questions when situations call for it.

Talk with an Attorney

Since legal issues have the potential to come up and if you're going to be in business for any length of time, they are almost a given. Therefore, you may want to consider having an attorney on file just in case. This may be important, especially if you are going to have high-end clients.

Get the Necessary Business Forms

Before you start, it is important to have several forms to use in your business. You will need work orders that outline what customers want to get done. Estimate forms for showing the price estimate to your customers for specific jobs. Cleaning invoice forms that describe the services you provided to the customer. Satisfaction survey forms for customers to detail how well you performed. Lastly, breakage report forms if something is broken in the customer's home.

If you are going to accept checks from customers, you should have some bad check notice forms on hand. In addition, if you foresee a need to hire independent contractors for certain jobs, you should have independent contractor forms that outline specific job responsibilities you are hiring someone to perform.

These forms should also have a statement that makes sure your independent contractor won't steal from customers. All forms should have a company name and logo. All forms, business cards, and advertising materials should have the same "branded" appearance. This provides your company with a professional appearance from the customer's point of view.

While you probably won't use all of these forms on a regular basis, it is a good idea to have them ready just in case. It is best to keep them in a downloadable format on your computer so you can print them whenever you need them.

Market and Promote Your New Business

The last step is also one of the most important steps in starting your residential cleaning business. No matter what type of service you are offering or your targeted market, you won't have a successful business if no one knows about it.

This means you need a good marketing plan in order to get the word out about your business. There are several ways to do this, and we'll cover them all in-depth later in this book.

Is Residential Cleaning Right For You?

As you can tell, there are many factors involved in starting a residential cleaning company. In addition to the step by step process listed above, you also need to make sure you have the skills needed to do the job, as we discussed earlier in this book.

Before you choose to start a residential cleaning business, you should ask yourself the following questions:

- Are you interested in making a full-time income while working part-time hours?
- Do you have the time and ability to start a business in two to three weeks before any income is earned?
- Are you willing and able to put forth at least $500 in capital to purchase the necessary cleaning equipment to start your business?
- Are you willing to start a new business while working from home in the evenings and/or on the weekends?
- Do you have the time and effort necessary to market and promote your business in order to build up an adequate client base?

By answering yes to the majority of these questions, you are likely in a good position to start a residential cleaning business. If this is the case, then keep reading to learn the specifics of starting and running your business so it can grow into a high-profit company for you.

10 Steps to Start a Commercial Cleaning Business

Whether you choose to start a commercial cleaning business first instead of a residential cleaning business or you choose to expand and start a commercial cleaning business after successfully establishing your residential cleaning business, there are a few things you need to do. There is a great demand for commercial cleaning, and it shares many of the benefits of residential cleaning.

Commercial cleaning differs from residential cleaning because it has higher contracts. A typical commercial contract can range between $1,000 and $3,000 per month. This means it can take less time to make a commercial cleaning business profitable than a residential cleaning business. Commercial cleaning is also fairly recession-proof.

While most of the steps for starting a commercial cleaning business are the same as starting a residential cleaning business, the process is a little different.

Let's take a look at the ten steps needed to start a commercial cleaning business.

Develop a Business Plan

As with any business, the first step is to get a solid business plan. At the very least this plan needs to include an overview of the company and the services you want to offer, the marketing strategy you plan to use to get customers, financial information including cash flow and income statements and an action plan for how your company is going to reach profit goals.

A business plan is basically considered a blueprint for success, so you should refer to it when you need to take action and accomplish things that help you start and grow your business.

Your business plan is also needed for banks or other lenders to review in case you need to apply for a business loan.

Come Up with a Business Name

If you are going to be cleaning commercial buildings, it is important that you have a good company name. As a commercial cleaning business, you want a professional name that also reflects the type of services you offer. This way, people will know exactly what type of commercial cleaning you do just by your name.

Determine Your Target Market

Since the commercial cleaning market is much broader than a residential cleaning market, it is important you identify your target market. Are you going to clean large office complexes or just small retail locations? Are you going to specialize in food production or government buildings? When you know your target market, you will be able to direct your marketing and advertising better.

In order to determine your target market, you should do a thorough assessment of the best possible customers for your services. Often the most common target areas include the following:

- Office Buildings
- Doctors Offices and Medical Buildings
- Insurance Agencies
- Companies in Strip Malls
- Retail Shops

It is usually a good idea to start small when you don't have a lot of employees. Then as you grow your company and hire additional employees, you can start expanding to bigger corporations and larger commercial cleaning accounts.

Setting Your Rates

As with residential cleaning, it is important that you have rates clearly established before starting your business. Again the main focus is going to be on expenses and time, just as they are with residential cleaning. However, for larger commercial jobs, it may be best to charge by the month.

Each commercial location is going to be different. So when setting your rates, you also need to take into account certain features such as type of floors, how many rooms, how many bathrooms, and a number of employees in the building.

Again you can contact commercial cleaning businesses in your area and get quotes from them to help you determine the best rate for your business. If you overcharge your customers, they will go to another company. On the other hand, if you undercut yourself, then you aren't making any profits.

Open a Business Bank Account

As with any new business, you want to have a separate bank account. Even if you are going to keep your business small, you want to keep your personal and business funds separate. Most banks and credit unions can help you in choosing and setting up a business bank account.

Obtain Licenses and Permits

This is the time when you need to make sure you've applied for all the necessary licenses and permits. You never want to find out later that your business has been operating illegally.

The jurisdiction you live in will have its own requirements, so you'll have to contact a county representative about the specific licenses and permits needed in your area. We'll discuss more about this in detail later.

Determine What Insurance You Need

Insurance is something you may need to run your business. This is sometimes more important for a commercial cleaning business since you are going into offices and other types of business establishments. There is the risk that someone could get injured or something could get broken.

You can talk with a local insurance agent in order to discuss your individual business needs to make sure you have adequate coverage before starting your company. It is always better to have insurance coverage and not need it rather than to find out later you are liable for an accident or injury.

If you are going to expand your business and hire employees, then you should also look into getting worker's compensation insurance coverage.

For a commercial cleaning business, it is also important to become bonded. You are going to be cleaning at office buildings where they are entrusting you with the keys to their business. When you are bonded, you are protected against employee theft. Again, your local liability insurance agent can help you with this, although we will also cover this later.

Be Prepared for Taxes

Once your company starts generating revenue, you are going to need to file business taxes. Unless you are comfortable doing this yourself, you should consider hiring an accountant or CPA to work with you from the moment you start your business.

It would also be a good idea to have a tax professional on hand to ask any questions or concerns you have regarding expenses, tax deductions, and other similar items throughout the year. An account can also help you with financial decisions throughout the year, such as the purchase of additional equipment, purchasing or leasing office space, and whether to start a retirement plan.

Be Prepared for Legal Issues

When dealing with commercial contracts, there is also an increased risk of dealing with legal issues. It depends on the commercial buildings you are cleaning and what you may come into contact with while cleaning. Therefore, it can be a really good idea to have an attorney on file to discuss legal issues.

Marketing & Promoting Your New Business

As with residential cleaning, the last step is also the most important. No matter what services you offer, you need to market your company, so people know your business exists.

When you have a good marketing plan, you will have a successful and profitable business. There are many marketing strategies you can take, and we'll discuss them in-depth later in this book.

Is Commercial Cleaning Business Right for You?

As with residential cleaning, before you get started, there are some questions you want to ask yourself to make sure commercial cleaning is right for you. Be sure to ask yourself the following:

- Are you ready to earn a full-time income by working part-time hours?
- Do you have the time and effort to get a business started in just a couple of weeks?
- Do you have a small amount of capital, around $500, to get started?
- Are you comfortable starting and growing a business from your home?
- Are you willing and able to do the marketing and promotion needed to build up a client base of commercial cleaning contracts?

When you answer yes to most of these questions, then you are likely ready to start your commercial cleaning business.

As you can tell, residential and commercial cleaning are very similar in the steps it takes to get started. So to avoid duplicating the information I give you, we'll go over some of the above areas in detail from the perspective of starting a cleaning business; the information can be applied to both a residential and a commercial cleaning business depending on what type you plan to start. If there is a difference, I'll mention it in the specific section. So let's get into the meat and potatoes of it now.

What You Need to Get Started

Perhaps one of the best things about a cleaning business is the fact that you don't need a lot of supplies to get started. All of your supplies will fit in any vehicle, and you probably won't need larger pieces of equipment and vehicles until you start taking on bigger projects.

For me, I started out with just a few supplies and grew once I have my first four or five accounts.

For residential cleaning, this is fine since you often bring the supplies with you to each job. Unless you have a few homeowners who have a specific type of cleaner they want you to use, one that they provide and keep at their home.

However, once you get commercial cleaning contracts, you may not want to bring supplies with you. Sometimes, you will only be cleaning the properties once a week or less. This means you are going to be carrying a lot of supplies with you, especially if it is a big property. For this reason, you may want to buy duplicates and keep them in a supply closet at the business if they have the space and room for this.

The most important thing is that you don't purchase any specific cleaning supplies until you are sure you have a contract. There's no use in spending money on supplies that you may not ever use.

You will also want to determine where to purchase your supplies. There are several options available, but I generally find a janitorial supply store to be best. I'll discuss this in detail later.

Cleaning Equipment You Will Need

In order to start a cleaning business, you are going to need the following items for both residential and commercial cleaning:

- A vacuum cleaner with attachments (for commercial cleaning you should consider a commercial-grade vacuum)
- Mop and bucket
- Dry mop
- Cloth rags
- Paper towels
- Toilet brush and toilet bowl cleaner
- Broom
- Dustpan and brush
- Rubber or latex gloves
- Cleaning products
- Furniture polish
- Garbage bags

For residential cleaning, you are going to also need a couple of dusters for low-level and high-level dusting. If you plan on doing any specialized floor care, you should have a steam cleaner. For commercial cleaning you are going to need the following additional pieces of equipment:

- Squeegee
- Floor Buffer
- Wet Floor Signs
- Extension Cords

For residential cleaning, you should have a good cart to carry everything in a while you take it to and from the job sites. Depending on the larger equipment needed for commercial cleaning, you will also need to get the appropriate vehicle to move your supplies to and from jobs.

Choosing the Right Vehicle

Cleaning job sites are going to be spread out across town and depending on the size of your city, maybe even through the county. You are going to need to get yourself and your supplies to and from your home or place of business.

You want a cost-effective and safe transportation option. Many cleaning professionals choose to use a cargo van, a minivan, or a pickup truck. The specific vehicle will depend on the equipment you are using and the distance you are traveling.

What to Look for When Buying a Vehicle

The most important thing to consider is how much equipment and supplies you will need to move from location to location. If you have just the basics, then a standard minivan or SUV will work well.

However, if you have heavy equipment such as floor machines, then you will not only need a vehicle that can support more weight, but also one that has a ramp or tailgate life so you can easily load and unload the equipment.

Safety Issues to Consider

Vans are often preferred to pickups since they are enclosed and can protect more expensive equipment from weather and theft. Vans also have a lower tailgate, which makes it easier to move equipment. Just remember to check weight limits before purchasing a vehicle. You don't want to purchase a vehicle that is undersized and unable to haul your required weight loads.

You also want to consider driver safety when purchasing a vehicle. Once you load your vehicle, you want to make sure that it has a way of securing chemicals and equipment, so they don't roll around or get pushed near the driver.

Most commercial vans have steel partitions or bulkheads that provide increased security by separating the cab from the cargo area. This will help keep things from shifting during transport.

If you have never driven a larger vehicle, you should do a test drive before making a purchase decision. There are going to be more blind spots with a larger vehicle, so you will have to rely on your side mirrors to navigate while driving. Most commercial vehicles have limited windows on both sides and rear.

Other Things to Consider

Before making a purchase, you also want to talk to your insurance agent about insurance costs. Commercial insurance is often more expensive than personal vehicle insurance, so you want to know this cost upfront, rather than be surprised later.

If your marketing focus is on green cleaning, then you don't want a gas-guzzling SUV. Showcase your green cleaning service by getting a fuel-efficient or hybrid vehicle.

Also, think about possible expansion. If you are going to grow your company later and need a fleet of vehicles, then you want to consider the color of the vehicle.

You want a common color that is easy to find later when you need to get additional fleet vehicles. White is often a good general color that also helps your colorful logo to stand out better.

After Your Purchase

Once you've purchased a vehicle for your company, you want to keep in mind the liability involved if someone gets into an accident. Have a policy for safety established, as well as maintenance and cleanliness.

Either you or someone within your company should be designated as the person to manage the fleet. This involves keeping each vehicle license, insurance, and registration up to date.

Maintain safety records, assign vehicle use, and authorize/issue fuel cards while inspecting mileage logs for accuracy. You should also make sure all company employees have a safe driving record.

Make sure all employees follow the rules and policies when driving the vehicles. This will have a positive impact on the reputation and public image of your company.

11 Steps for Choosing Cleaning Products and Equipment

When it comes to choosing equipment and supplies for your cleaning business, you want to choose cleaning equipment that is inexpensive, accurate, and effective. Choosing your cleaning equipment is the very first and most important decision you will make when starting a cleaning business.

For the last ten years that I've been in business, I've been through the selection process quite a bit. There is a lot that you need to consider to make sure you are getting the best products and equipment to complete the task. You want to achieve cleaning results while also complying with regulations and keeping your costs in check.

In addition, it's hard not to go to the store and be faced with an advertisement for some new product that claims to do a better job than the product you're currently using. Figuring out a product doesn't need to be complicated, but you do need to do some research and gain some data in order to determine if a product is right for you. Let's look at ten steps you can take to decide what products and equipment are best for your company.

1. Look for an SDS - Safety Data Sheet

This is an important aspect of all cleaning supplies. The Safety Data Sheets or SDS used to be called Material Safety Data Sheets or MSDS; the term was revised in 2012. Why are these sheets so important? Legally, if the manufacturer doesn't have an SDS, then you aren't supposed to use it for your cleaning services. You can read more about this requirement in the OSHA Hazard Communication Standard. You'll want to maintain a master SDS binder in the business office or at your home. You can also go high-tech and have all the sheets in an MS Word or PDF file.

2. Does It Work?

Now we get to the product and one of the most time consuming and effort taking parts of the process. However, once you do this step, everything else is faster and easier. When doing a product test, you want to use exact measurements and observe dwell times in order to get a fair comparison of various products.

For simple cleaning, not including sanitizing or disinfecting, you want to record the following information:

- Dilution
- Application
- Dwell Time
- Rinsing Procedures
- Dry Time

To test truly test for sanitizing and disinfecting results, you would need to do laboratory testing. However, a good alternative is to use an ATP testing system. These can be a bit expensive, so if your clients want true sanitizing and disinfecting, this would be one of those extra charges for clients. Swab the surface with the test and measure the bio-load present.

Then follow the instructions on the product: using exactly the right dilution, pre-cleaning, dwell time, and rinse/dry time. Then swab and re-measure the bioload remaining.

While it can be expensive to do this at home for purposes of testing, don't hang on to supplies that don't do a good job the first time in completely or dramatically reducing the bioload. Rather, try different products and compare the measurements to make sure you get good results.

3. How Time Efficient Is the Product

While testing the product, you should also keep track of how long it takes to achieve the advertised performance. Then you know how long all your products take together for the entire cleaning procedure.

Using the data from step 2, compare your options. Products that work and those that work within a good time frame can stay in your inventory while other products are discarded. Even if a product works well, you won't save any money if it takes too long to accomplish goals. In fact, the cost of labor may mean a product that takes longer to complete costs more.

Always keep in mind that you may sometimes find a single product to replace two or more products you currently use. On the other hand, you may also find two products that work better or faster than a single one you currently use. Test each product separately and then compare everything and assess how they will fit in with your cleaning routine.

4. Support of Business and Safety Philosophies

To a certain extent, the products you use will reflect your business philosophy and promote the services you offer. This is especially important if you choose to advertise using the specific products you offer to clients.

For example, if you offer green cleaning, then all your supplies should be green in nature. If you think from this perspective, you can narrow your product options before you even start testing products.

Some cleaning companies will go so far as to develop and manufacture their own homemade cleaning products. If you choose to do this, you need to make sure you are operating within OSHA regulations, as stated in the Communication Hazard Standard.

5. You Get What You Pay For

Most cleaning products come in two primary forms: diluted and concentrated. Diluted or ready-to-use products are the primary items you find in stores, and these are often very economical for professional cleaners. However, this is because you are paying for 90% water. On the other hand, this is the best option if you want to avoid dilution steps or errors.

It can be a better idea to avoid paying for diluted products and just buy concentrated solutions. With this option, there are two types. The first is portion packs that are pre-measured, so you can easily mix them at the job site. The second is dilution systems that are kept at your home or retail location, and you have to properly and consistently mix the right amounts with water.

You can compare the cost of these two solutions very easily. To compare diluted and concentrated prices, divide the price you pay by the number of diluted ounces. Now you can get a fair estimate of which is more cost-effective for you.

6. Where to Purchase

While we will discuss where to purchase products later, the main point to understand here is that you want a product that is easy to access. You want reliable access to your chosen product while able to get it at a price that fits within your budget. You don't want to spend time testing and training employees on a product only to be unable to find it.

7. Evaluating Cleaning Equipment

Evaluating cleaning equipment involves the same basic steps as a cleaning or disinfecting product. So when it comes to cleaning equipment, use steps 2 to 4 above to start: product testing, time, and safety/philosophy.

If a piece of equipment claims to disinfect, then you want to check for an EPA Registration Number, which is the legal authorization for this to make such a claim. Then, you can look at more equipment specific aspects in order to determine the best option for your cleaning business.

8. Warranty

Equipment warranties are very important since they can save you a lot of money on basic repairs through part or all of the lifetime of the device.

Be sure to look at equipment reviews from a number of websites to get a feel for how the manufacturer handles any warranty issues. Ideally, the manufacturer should handle issues quickly, efficiently, and with little hassle.

9. Supply and Maintenance Costs

Go to the manufacturer's website and review the care and maintenance requirements carefully. Draft a quick schedule for expected replacements and calculate the costs of these extras beyond the initial cost of the equipment.

For example, a vacuum is going to need filters, belts, and hoses on occasion. Again, you can turn to product reviews for a good expectation of when these ongoing costs are going to happen.

10. Cost Through the Warranty Period Compared with the Cost of Others

Check to see what ongoing costs are included in the equipment warranty. This way, you can possibly subtract some of the costs from your overall expenses or investment.

11. Expected Life of the Equipment

The equipment manufacturer should be able to tell you the expected life of each piece of equipment, especially commercial line products. The expected life is the average number of months or years a piece of equipment is expected to achieve advertised results. However, not all cleaning equipment is measured in months or years. Consider the following guidelines for some of the most common life estimates of cleaning equipment:

- **Cotton or Microfiber Cloths** - These are measured in the number of washes. A cloth that lasts 250 washes is going to last about a year while a cloth with 500 washes will last about two years, assuming you use and wash your cloths each day.
- **Residential Vacuums** - These are measured in years, based on once a week use. So a residential model with a useful life of five years might last a professional residential cleaning company for about one and a half years if you use it at three homes a day.
- **Commercial Vacuums** - Again, measured in years, based on continuous use several times a day. This is why commercial vacuums, although more expensive upfront, are more cost-effective as an investment because you spend less money over time.

5 Types of Cleaners

There is no shortage of cleaners on the market, but you aren't going to use most of them. Rather there are only five specific types of cleaners that a professional cleaning business is going to use. Let's consider the most common types of cleaners that you will use and what you should know about them.

Neutral Cleaner

This is typically found in all-purpose cleaners or a neutral floor cleaner. Neutral refers to the number 7 on the pH scale. Most neutral cleaners aren't really 7 but can range from 6.25 to 8.25 on the pH scale. Neutral cleaners are often safe on most surfaces that are water washable, without damaging any protective coatings. These are best for daily light-duty cleaning.

All-Purpose Cleaner

An all-purpose cleaner, like a neutral cleaner, can be used for most water washable surfaces such as countertops. However, these can't be used on floors with a finish. This is because most all-purpose cleaners are on the alkaline side of the pH scale, meaning they are 9 to 11. The alkaline chemical can harm the floor finish.

Glass Cleaner

As the name implies, this is often used for glass and mirrors. Although it can also be used for bright-work such as faucets and other similar stainless steel or chrome finish materials. Glass cleaners often contain solvents such as alcohol or ammonia as well as low levels of non-volatile solvents. This is a good combination for removing oily soil, such as fingerprints, and also prevents streaking.

Acid Cleaner

Acid cleaners are best for the tough mineral deposits found in restrooms. You need to be careful when using these cleaners since they can damage the surface you are cleaning and can also be dangerous to humans if the proper protection isn't used. Always wear gloves and eye protection with these cleaners. You should also avoid inhaling fumes since they can damage the lungs. Read the manufacturer's instructions for proper protection. Hydrochloric acid cleaners should only be used for toilet bowls. Phosphoric acid cleaners can be used on other surfaces that require acid treatment, but again you should follow the manufacturer's instructions to ensure safe use.

Degreasers

If you can't get the job done with all-purpose cleaners or neutral cleaners, then you may need to use a heavy-duty degreaser. These cleaners use solvents or alkaline builders to help remove grease and oils from most surfaces.

Choosing the Best Vacuum

One of the most commonly used pieces of equipment in the cleaning business is the vacuum. When you go to make this purchase, you will be faced with dozens of choices. While the choosing process can seem daunting, you can make the process easier by choosing one that has the features you need for a professional cleaning business. Consider the following when choosing the right vacuum:

- Weight - Nothing wears down faster than a heavy vacuum cleaner. Also, lightweight vacuums are easier to handle and place less strain on your arms and back.
- Ergonomic - A vacuum should have an ergonomic and lightweight handle, so it is easy

to maneuver without straining your hands and forearm.
- Tools - A vacuum with built-in, easy-to-reach tools is going to make your job easier.
- Cords - The longer the cord, the better, ideally it should be about fifty feet.
- Parts and Accessories - Make sure it is easy to buy or order the necessary parts and accessories, while also comparing the price of these.
- Filters - For indoor air quality, it is important to choose a vacuum that uses micro-filter bags or HEPA filters. Be sure to check prices since sometimes a HEPA filter may cost more than a bag.
- Brush Speed - The ideal speed is 4000+ rpm in order to remove all dirt and soil from the carpet.
- Amps - Don't get too focused on the amps of a vacuum. This refers to the energy used but doesn't really have any impact on the performance of the vacuum.
- Motors - The ideal vacuum will have two motors. While this may seem like just another part to go out, it can actually make your vacuum more efficient. One motor will create the suction while the other motor rotates the brush. These vacuums will have more productivity since they pick up more soil.
- Design - Make sure your vacuum is able to get under furniture and easily vacuum close to walls, eliminating the amount of accessory work you have to do with the vacuum.

Mop Buckets and Wringers

    This may not seem like a big deal since a mop is a mop after all, but the most important thing to choose is the right bucket and wringer.

- Metal Buckets and Wringers - These last a long time, are very durable, and are rust-resistant too. Steel handles for the wringers also mean you can apply added pressure when wringing a mop.
- Plastic Buckets - These are the most commonly chosen since they are lightweight, durable, and affordable. You can get them in sizes ranging from 20 to 50 gallons. The plastic buckets come with either side-press or down-press wringers.
  - Down-Press Wringers - These use a downward action to wring mops. When you press down from the top, you are able to put extra pressure on the mop.
  - Side-Press Wringers - This places pressure on the mop from the side. You need to use extra force with these wringers.
- Duo Buckets - These have two tanks. You will usually use one tank for your mopping solution and the other from a rinsing solution. Often these buckets are for cleaning in healthcare facilities and may include antimicrobial agents to help resist bacterial growth.
- Strainer Mop Buckets - These are made from very lightweight plastic, which is great if you need to go up and down stairs, but they often have a low gallon capacity.
- Microfiber Mop Buckets - These are designed for the newer microfiber mop pads. They have a press sieve, which allows for no-touch removal of cleaning solution from mops. They

are durable because they have no moving parts and non-marking casters.

Choosing the Right Dusting Tools

I know it seems silly that I'm talking about choosing a dusting tool. After all, they all work the same, right? This is where you would be wrong. There are a number of dusters on the market, and one of the most common complaints among customers is dusting. So it is important you take the time to consider the right dusting tool for the job.

Whether residential or commercial, dusting is a time-consuming task. Not all dusting equipment is the same, and you need to choose the best tool to accomplish and reduce the time this task takes. The most common dusters include the following:

- Feather
- Synthetic
- Microfiber
- Extension
- Lambswool
- Pipe
- Hand
- Counter
- Split
- Impregnated Disposable Dust Cloths
- Dusting Attachments for the Vacuum Cleaner

These are just the main categories; each also has subtypes filled with more specialized dusters.

Buying a duster is a lot more than simply choosing between a few options.

Choosing the right duster is a matter of what you plan to use it for. If you are dusting a small, confined area like a desktop or mantel, then a Lambswool or a microfiber duster would be ideal, but if you are dusting wide open and expansive areas, then you may need the commercial-grade disposable type dusters.

Also, consider the area you are dusting in - a home with little traffic or an office near a manufacturing plant with a lot of thick dust on a daily basis. Is there a high ceiling or exposed pipes in the ceiling? These are just a few of the considerations when choosing a duster to use.

Again, just because a specific category of duster works doesn't mean you can use just any type of duster. For example, a feather duster is quite common, but there are a variety of types. Most feather dusters are made from ostrich features, but the quality varies whether it is black, gray, or floss ostrich feathers.

You can use turkey feather dusters in place of ostrich to save money. The difference is that real dusters clean with tiny barbs on the feathers that grab the dust and hold it. Cheaper quality feather dusters use static electricity to clean dust.

For commercial cleaning, lambswool dusters are often preferred. Another good option is treated with disposable dust sleeves that fit over the dusters and allow them to last longer. Sleeves that are made of microfiber are a good choice since they are durable, washable and can last for years when you take care of them.

Synthetic, pipe, and split dusters are good when you need a particular shape for dusting. Most work using the static electricity method to collect dust and come with extension handles to reach high surfaces.

The current trend for cleaning businesses is to use microfiber cloths. These have many uses and are often color-coded, so you can designate them for specific functions. You can use them wet or dry and wash them over and over again.

Lastly, there is the option of using a vacuum cleaner attachment. This is useful for high dusting, getting into tight areas, or to ensure dust doesn't enter the air. This is good when you don't want dust to be airborne.

As you can tell, there are many types of dusters to choose from depending on your circumstances. You want one that is effective and efficient. Perhaps you can have a few on hand to do whatever job you need. Since dusting is a common complaint area, it wouldn't be a bad idea to be prepared.

Where to Buy Cleaning Supplies

As you can tell, there are a lot of supplies and equipment needed to run a cleaning business.

So, where can you go to get all these things for your business?

You can do your shopping at various local stores, or you can go to a janitorial distributor. Personally, I like to get my supplies from a janitorial distributor.

First, let me tell you about some of the other options, and then I'll tell you the benefits I enjoy from getting my supplies from a janitorial distributor.

Retail Stores

Grocery stores and home good stores are a great source of diluted cleaning products. You have multiple locations to choose from, so it is quick and easy to get what you need. However, when you buy this way, it is also the most expensive, and preferred products can disappear as the stock is adjusted.

Wholesale Clubs

Some club stores are starting to make an effort to sell more to professionals by offering larger size products, concentrates, and refillable bottles. However, as with retail stores, the products they carry can change quickly or available for only a few months out of the year. Prices are often lower, but you won't get any training, support, or SDS sheets.

If something goes wrong with the equipment, you will have to send it back to the manufacturer for service or repairs, which means it takes longer to get your equipment back when something goes wrong.

Online Stores

The internet is full of stores where you can buy both common and specialty cleaning products. You can even get some decent discounts at online stores. Just take some precautions to make sure you are purchasing through a legitimate business. Online shopping also makes it easier to compare prices.

No matter where you choose to buy from, it is important to plan ahead and make sure you have all of the supplies and equipment you need. Where you buy your supplies won't necessarily harm your business, but having a dependable source certainly makes it easier. This is why I prefer a janitorial distributor for my supplies.

Why Buy from Janitorial Distributors

High-quality cleaning supplies and equipment are necessary for you and your employees to do the job effectively. A janitorial supplies distributor can provide you with professional products and much more. At first, buying from a janitorial distributor may seem to cost more; but the products are higher quality, so they are more efficient and clean better. Consider some of the benefits you get from buying through a janitorial distributor:

- You can get products in concentrated form, meaning a small amount goes a long way. This means you are actually spending less than if you buy from a retailer.
- Many janitorial distributors will sometimes offer quantity discounts when you make high volume purchases.
- Distributors maintain records for you so you can have a resource for warranty information.
- Distributors are able to provide you with SDS sheets. Since you are required to have SDS sheets for all your cleaning chemicals, this is certainly easier than having to go online to find them.
- Distributors have in-depth product knowledge. This means they can make recommendations for suitable products based on your particular situation. They will also know if a lower priced product is just as good as a higher-priced item.
- Some distributors will also be able to train you and your employees on how to use new products or equipment. This can help make

your staff more efficient. This saves you money in labor savings.
- Depending on the distributor you purchase from, they may have repair services on-site, so you don't have to worry about sending the equipment back to the manufacturer for repairs.
- If you need a specialized product, then the distributor can suggest products, and if they don't have it, they should know where to order it from.

Pricing alone isn't the only factor when buying cleaning supplies. With a janitorial distributor, you may not be saving a lot on the cost of supplies, but the experience and other benefits you are getting are just as valuable. So, in my opinion, I say it is best to buy from a janitorial distributor, but do what you find is best for your cleaning business.

Legal Requirements

Before you can start a cleaning business, you need to be considered a legal entity. This includes choosing a business name and then registering your business.

In addition, there is licensing and bonding, plus insurance to consider. In order to do a lot of this, you will need to set up a business structure.

Let's take a look at some of the legal requirements you need to consider in order to get your cleaning business started properly.

Registering a Cleaning Business

The first step you need to take in starting a cleaning business is to register it with the state and the county where you are going to operate your business. To do this, you need to have a business name and identify a business structure.

Contact the county clerk's office, city hall, or the department in charge of business licensing. Find out from them if you need to obtain an occupational license or if you simply need to register a DBA or Doing Business As with the local government. Each city and county are different.

Contact the secretary of state where you are opening your cleaning business. Tell them the name of the business entity you are registering. They will provide you with an application and a list of any other documents you need in order to register your business successfully.

For example, corporations will need to write and submit the articles of incorporation in order to register a business.

Lastly, register with the Internal Revenue Service. On the federal level, you also need to register with the IRS for tax purposes. If you are going to employ individuals, then you need to apply for an Employer Identification Number. Some businesses will need only a Tax Identification Number, which is the same as a social security number of a business.

Business Structure

When starting a house cleaning business, there are five different business structures you can choose from:

1. Sole Proprietor
2. Partnership
3. Corporation (Inc. or Ltd.)
4. S Corporation
5. Limited Liability Company (LLC)

Sole Proprietor

This is the most common structure for a cleaning business. It is used for a business owned by a single person or a married couple. Under this structure, the owner is personally liable for all business debts and may file on their personal income tax.

Partnership

This is another inexpensive business structure to form. It often requires an agreement between two or more individuals who are going to own and operate a business jointly. The partners will share all aspects of the business in accordance with the agreement.

Partnerships don't pay taxes, but they need to file an informational return. Individual partners then report their share of profits and losses on their personal tax returns.

Corporation (Inc. or Ltd.)

This is one of the more complex business structures and has the most startup costs of any business structure. It isn't a very common structure among cleaning businesses since there are shares of stocks involved. Profits are taxed both at the corporate level and again when distributed to shareholders. When you structure a business at this level, there are often lawyers involved.

S Corporation

This is one of the most popular types of business entity people form to avoid double taxation. It is taxed similar to a partnership entity.

But an S Corp. needs to be approved to be classified as such, so it isn't very common among cleaning businesses.

Limited Liability Company (LLC)

This is the second most common business structure among cleaning businesses. It offers benefits for small businesses since it reduces the risk of losing all your personal assets in case you are faced with a lawsuit. It provides a clear separation between business and personal assets. You can also elect to be taxed as a corporation, which saves you money come tax time.

If you are unsure which specific business structure you should choose, then you can discuss it with an accountant. They will direct you in the best possible option for what your business goals are.

Do You Need to Become Bonded?

This is one of the biggest questions and often one of the most confusing for cleaning business owners. Since most of the general public is confused as well, it means most think business owners need to be bonded. Bonding protects your cleaning business against employee theft.

If you don't have employees, you don't need to be bonded. However, many choose to purchase it since it can be used as a marketing tool and makes homeowners more comfortable when hiring you for residential cleaning.

You can purchase bonds through insurance companies. You can also protect yourself by having a clause in your contract for homeowners to remove all sentimental and valuable items as your company isn't responsible for lost or broken items.

You can get a $10,000 bond for about $300 per year, but the benefit of using the word "bonded" can be very helpful in your marketing campaign when you are trying to establish yourself as a professional cleaning business.

Do I Need a Business License?

This is another confusing part. Often a cleaning business doesn't require a "trade business license," but most states/countries will require you to register your business with a local government office. It varies widely from state to state, so it is a good idea to make a call to your local city business license office and ask what type of license is required for your business. But I assure you, it will not be something expensive.

How to Become Licensed and Bonded

While most states don't consider cleaning to be a regulated profession and there are no rules that say a cleaning business needs to be licensed and bonded; doing so can demonstrate your professionalism and commitment to quality service.

Being licensed shows customers that you are following the law and have appropriate government permissions to provide cleaning services. Bonding protects the customers by guaranteeing the job will be completed, or they will receive adequate compensation. While it isn't that difficult or expensive to obtain the proper licensing and bonding, you will need to start early since it requires time for approval of several applications.

Your local city, county, and state government will be able to provide you information about licensing laws in your area as well as requirements and procedures.

Some locations require cleaning businesses to be licensed as service contractors, while others only require a general business license. Also, some locations require you to hold a certain amount of insurance in order to file for a surety bond prior to being licensed.

You can purchase a professional bond from your insurance agent. The amount of your bond will depend on the size and scope of your cleaning business as well as local regulations. Often bonds cover about $2,000 to $10,000 of customer reimbursement for an independent contractor or small service business.

Once you are licensed and bonded, be sure to include your license number on all advertisements, business cards, contracts, invoices, and any other official correspondence so customers will be able to verify your license. You should also note in your service agreements or contracts that you are a bonded cleaning business and provide customers with information about whom to contact in the event that a job isn't completed and how they can seek reimbursement.

Should You Get Insurance?

Personally, I feel insurance is not only important but essential for your business. If you have a business, you want to cover yourself and your client's property. Insurance isn't that expensive, and it may make a big difference in your business, not to mention the peace of mind it will provide for you in the long run.

Many people are leery of allowing strangers into their homes, especially if they aren't going to be there. If you don't have adequate coverage or don't run your business in a professional manner, then you are less likely to be hired.

One of the best things a client looks for besides experience is insurance. They want to make sure their property is covered in case something happens. Talk with an insurance agent to get information on how much coverage you should get.

What is CIMS?

The Cleaning Industry Management Standard (CIMS) is a certification program developed over three years ago by the International Sanitary Supply Association (ISSA) along with the American Institute of Cleaning Science (AICS). In the three years since its development, they have certified over 140 organizations and businesses as being in compliance with the requirements of the standard.

Why Get Certified?

Getting certified through CIMS will provide you with a number of benefits. In order to get the most return on investment with CIMS, you need to go the extra mile. Not only will you enjoy many benefits, but it also provides additional proof to customers that your cleaning business stands out from the rest.

What It Includes

CIMS is based on six best practice management principles built around the foundations of success and improvement in any organization or business:

1. Quality Systems
2. Service Delivery

3. Human Resource
4. Health, Safety and Environmental Stewardship
5. Management Commitment
6. Green/Sustainable Building Cleaning Practices

Each business needs to meet or exceed the requirements of the CIMS standard. Each assessment involves an assessor going through a CIMS checklist of about 130 items. The items on the checklist are designed to validate the required documentation and processes for a cleaning business.

This means that a cleaning business needs to have documents, procedures, and policies that are actually being used in the day to day operation of the business. If the application you submit also wants to get Green Building endorsement, then there are another 105 requirements that need to be met.

An assessment starts at your corporate office or home business with documents being reviewed, and questions asked. Then the assessment will move to account locations or buildings in order to verify that documents and processes are in place and being followed. This part of the assessment involves talking to cleaners, supervisors, customers, and the supply distributor.

After the assessment, a meeting with key staff members is done for a debriefing session. During this session, the findings, observations, and recommendations for improvements are discussed.

If the minimum requirements aren't met, and the deficiencies are only minor, then the assessor may guide the business in meeting the requirements.

If this isn't possible, then a re-visit needs to be scheduled. A recertification audit is scheduled every two years in order to ensure that the standards are being maintained.

Benefits of CIMS Certification

When your business is CIMS certified, the process provides a focus for the business that results in unexpected cohesion and synergy of all staff members. This includes breaking down barriers between departments, locations, and shifts.

CIMS also provides a foundation for ongoing process and quality improvement within a cleaning business. It also allows a cleaning business to take themselves to higher levels of quality, efficiency, and profit.

CIMS certification can provide you with a way to get ahead of your competition. In addition, while getting certified, you are able to use the documentation you compile to make marketing and sales tools.

CIMS certification will open new markets for you and will allow you to compete in a broader market when a contract specifically requires a third party, green or CIMS certifications.

When compiling documentation for CIMS certification, you can develop a framework for the company and department-wide standardization, consistency, and management control.

This is often the first time the business is organized and has all of the operational documents in one place for easy access and revision. In itself, this improves efficiency and cost savings.

Establishing a Residential Cleaning Rate Structure

The most common question among those starting a cleaning business is what to set the rate structure at.

One thing I need to state upfront is that you should never give a quote over the phone. Rather, tell them you can give them a general idea of what to expect, but you can't give an accurate quote until you are able to look at the home.

There are several variables you have to take into consideration when quoting a price for residential cleaning, including the following:

- Size of the home
- Number of bathrooms
- Condition of home
- Pets
- Frequency of cleaning
- Number of people in the home
- Whether cleaning supplies are provided
- Additional services requested that aren't in the basic cleaning

Once you have seen the home and know exactly what the clients want to have done, then you can give them a per-job rate. You shouldn't quote an hourly rate at first.

Often you are going to need to do an initial clean. This is to make sure the home gets to your standards and will require some maintenance cleaning. From there, the client can schedule a cleaning service either weekly, bi-weekly, or even monthly. Initial cleanings are often a bit more expensive than maintenance cleanings.

Depending on the size and condition of the home, they can range from $100-$200. Make sure you factor in how many hours the first clean will take you, then how many hours your maintenance cleanings will take.

Always make sure you charge enough to make the job worth it. Undercharging will often lead to cutting corners and giving subpar service. Once you have an initial clean quote, you can give them that along with their regular cleaning rate. Often maintenance cleanings will be $20-$35 per hour depending on the job. Let's look a little more closely at how you can determine your maintenance rate.

How to Charge

Remember, when setting the hourly rate, that you need to charge a little more than what you want to take home. This allows you to cover the cost of materials and other overhead expenses. The hourly rate can be used as a baseline for determining the entire cost you charge the customer.

You can determine what to charge on top of your hourly rate by looking at past overhead expenses. If you are new to the residential cleaning business, then you can research the averages for the industry. Overhead is often low, especially if you are based out of your home. Some examples of overhead would include the cost of driving to and from your house, the cost of printing advertisements and invoices, and any utility costs such as phone and internet service.

You can choose to charge a flat rate rather than by the hour. However, you often make less money when you charge a flat rate rather than by the house. One house can take an hour to clean while a similar house of the same size can take five hours to clean. However, if you are cleaning less than an hour, it may be necessary to charge a flat rate.

You also need to decide how you are going to charge customers for the cleaning supplies you use. Equipment such as vacuums, mops, and brooms can be a part of your overhead expenses since they last longer and are reused. On the other hand, you can charge cleaning supplies such as bleach and ammonia as materials since you will need to replenish them after each job, and the amount you use will be determined by the size of the job.

Add the cost of overhead and supplies to your base hourly rate. Usually, this is done as a percentage. For example, your overhead expenses and cost of materials may total five percent of your labor costs. In this case, you will add five percent to your base hourly rate.

Now you can type up an invoice to present to the customer at the end of each job or within a week of completing the job. Clearly show the costs to the customer, such as rate per hour and any extra costs for additional supplies or surcharge for extra services.

Include any details a customer may need to know on the invoice, such as when payment is expected and if there is a penalty for late payment. If this is the case, clearly state the penalty amount and when it is applied. Then, at that time, send another invoice with the new amount to the customer.

Establish a Commercial Cleaning Rate Structure

When you first start a commercial cleaning business, it can be a bit difficult to determine how much you should charge for your services. For commercial cleaning services, there are several factors to take into consideration so you can charge the appropriate amount.

The Supply and Demand Theory

For commercial cleaning, you first want to look at the supply and demand in your area. If you are the only business offering commercial cleaning, then you can basically determine your own rates and see who is willing to pay them. However, you are likely not the only commercial cleaning business in the area, so you won't be able to charge as much money.

Competitive Pricing

You should pay attention to what other commercial cleaning businesses are charging in your area. Call your competitors and ask for a quote.

You can then price accordingly. You don't want to charge more than your competitors. Otherwise, your customers are going to go with your competitors in order to save money. On the other hand, you don't want to charge so low that it isn't profitable for you.

Contracts and One-Time Jobs

For commercial cleaning services, you need to have a rate structure for contract jobs and a separate one for one-time cleaning jobs.

For example, cleaning a large business three times a week is going to be priced less than doing just a one-time cleaning job. You should always charge less if you are going to be getting more work from the customer regularly.

Pricing

Pricing for commercial cleaning can vary greatly depending on the location and the type of cleaning that needs to be done. For example, you may charge only $20 or $30 a visit for a small office.

If you are cleaning a large office building several times a week with just basic cleaning, then you may charge something like $500 to $700 a month. For very large jobs, it may be best to quote by the square foot. The average figure would be about $0.5 to $0.10 per square foot. You will also want to charge for any specialized cleaning tasks or services.

How to Bid and Win Contracts

When you run a cleaning business, bidding on potential accounts is one of the most important and yet most misunderstood aspects. Even when people know about it, it is also the most feared part of the process.

Even after ten years of operating a cleaning business, bidding is still a difficult and challenging aspect of running my own business.

10 Tips for Better Bidding

Let me give you some tips on how to make bidding on projects more successful and less stressful.

Success in bidding is based on four principles:

1. Professionalism
2. Accuracy
3. Marketing
4. Competitiveness

1. Listen to the Customer

Takes notes and listen to the customer; this shows you are respecting them and interested in what they are saying while also helping you to focus on the customer's primary concerns and problem areas.

Most cleaning businesses run into issues when they don't pay attention to the small details, which turn into big issues. Don't lose details by only listening; write things down on paper. Get all the facts by asking the necessary questions. All this information will also help you to bid accurately, perform according to the customer's expectations, and make a decent profit.

2. Read the Contract, Specifications, and Request for Proposals

If the customer gives you a contract, written specifications, or a request for proposals, take the time to read them carefully. Going over everything in detail, make notes in the margins about any concerns you have and ask any questions you need for clarification.

For smaller jobs, the customers are less likely to have things prepared for you. Some customers would even prefer not to have a contract. If a customer asks for a contract, they are often only expecting a simple one, two, or three-page specification, and a work agreement.

On the other hand, for larger corporations, you can expect sophisticated documentation that is sometimes sixty pages or more and includes blueprints and legal requirements.

3. Walk the Property

Never assume the information you are given is correct. Rather go to the property and measure, verify, look, ask, and inventory in order to get correct information about the area you will be cleaning. You can determine square footage through electronic measuring devices or a rolling wheel.

It is your responsibility to know the job before bidding. If you go back later to ask for more money or to complain that you didn't get adequate information makes you look incompetent and starts the business relationship off wrong.

When touring the building open all doors and ask questions when you have them. Look in the janitor closets for what supplies are provided. Inventory square footage based on floor types. Carefully note any specific problems, areas, or requirements so you can ask the customer how these should be handled both in the contract and once you start service. Point out to them if something is considered an extra service or is included in the basic service.

Also, keep in mind how you plan to staff the project and what types of equipment and supplies you will need. Again, make notes for references later so you can save both time and money by not having to go back repeatedly in order to gather additional information.

While this all takes a lot of time, it will show the customer that you are a professional who knows what they're doing and is prepared to provide the level of service they expect.

The main focus is to bid accurately, satisfy the customer, and make a decent profit while also knowing what is required and expected of you. You want to know all of this before you place your bid.

4. Cut Costs, Improve Quality and Share the Savings

The cleaning business is very competitive. Companies are cutting back, downsizing, and looking for ways to reduce costs. As the cleaning business providing a service to them, you need to do the same. However, this doesn't mean you need to reduce the quality or level of service. Rather consider looking at the following areas:

- Efficiency - Find better and faster ways to do the work while still getting the same or improved results.
- Frequency - Be realistic. Are there some things that can be done less frequently without compromising quality, safety, appearance, or health?
- Wasted Time - Make sure all employees have specific duties along with time expectations. If you give employees too much time to finish a task, they'll either slow down or find other things to do. Labor accounts for 90% of your costs, so labor efficiency is very important.
- Specify Procedures - You should have written procedures that tell and show employees how you expect each task to be done, how long it will take, and what the expected results are going to be. Basic instructions aren't useful. Provide employees with initial and on-going training, so employees always know how to do their job and what they are expected to do.
- Equipment Savings - Can you reduce labor hours by using an auto-scrubber or a larger vacuum? Use a cart in order to cut down on the number of trips. Any equipment that reduces time and labor costs is a worthwhile investment.
- Preventative Measures - You don't need to clean items as frequently if they don't get dirty. Use walk-off mats at entrances and sweep, vacuum or hose these frequently in order to

avoid tracked soil. Place trash cans where they are easy for people to use.
- The Right Attitude - Keep an eye out for ways that you can cut costs while improving quality. This helps you to keep a competitive edge. You can develop it into an expectation and a way of doing business.
- Pass on the Savings - When you find a way to save money, share it with your customers and employees. While this may seem contrary to short-term business thinking, this is actually becoming the way of the future. When you pass along savings, your customers are more likely to stay loyal and your employees happy. There is a lot of competition in the cleaning business, and this allows you to provide something extra for customers and/or employees.

5. Innovative Approaches

This can vary based on the situation, so you need to try and find new or different ways of doing work. To achieve success and retain it, you need to take some risks and stay at the forefront of technology, procedures, and management philosophies.

In today's competitive business cleaning marketplace, change is the only constant. Embrace this and accept the challenge by using it to find a better, more economical way to serve your customers.

6. Respond to the Specifications and Contract; Offer Additional Options

Give your customers what they ask for, but then go a step further by offering some other options that can help them save money and make your bid more attractive than the competition. This not only keeps your bid competitive, but it also puts you in a position where you can negotiate. Some options to consider include:

- Pulling items/tasks out of the bid
- Changing the frequency of certain tasks
- Recommending new equipment, procedures or products
- Implement a recycling program
- Interim carpet cleaning/spotting

7. Triple Check Bid Calculations

Errors are unacceptable in business; they mean the difference between profit and loss. The larger the job, the greater the risk involved. Errors will cause you to look unprofessional, can cost you a cleaning account, and in some cases, even your business. In order to assure accuracy, triple check your figures and then have someone else check your calculations and proofread what you have written.

8. Realistic Expectation of Job Ability

Business growth should be done slowly, one step at a time. Be realistic that you can't provide everything to everyone. Define a realistic service area, target a specific size and type of account. Define a specialty and strive to be the best service contractor in the country every day.

Don't waste your time and a customer's by going after accounts that you can't handle. This applies to the size, location, and types of services provided.

9. Sell Quality Service at a Fair Price

In the cleaning business, quality is the key to long-term success. A good reputation helps you to sell and win contracts. A bad reputation can take years of hard work to overcome. You need profitable accounts that allow you to pay your bills, pay yourself a decent salary, and have enough left over to reinvest in business growth. You can't afford to hold on to accounts that are financial losses unless there is a good reason; public relations or expectation of profit in the long-term. See the earlier segment on pricing and charging to make sure you are quoting a fair price.

10. Reinvest

The first step is to reinvest in yourself. You can't afford to fall behind in the times, and things are changing every day. While you can't know everything, you can constantly seek new knowledge. The most important thing is to know where to go for answers when you need them. As a business owner, you should subscribe to and read at least two or three industry magazines while attending as many seminars and conventions as you can. When you follow these guidelines, along with hard work and quality service, you will be able to increase your chances of success.

The second step is to reinvest in your business. You should always have some money to put back into the business. Buy new equipment, pay better wages and benefits, computerize, and set aside a certain amount for advertising and promotion.

The third is to reinvest in the industry. Join and be a part of cleaning industry trade associations. There are 40 such groups throughout the United States, and many have local chapters in metropolitan areas. When you join these associations, you enjoy a number of advantages, making it well worth the cost. You can discuss innovative methods, evaluate new products, and be aware of new trends.

Lastly, you want to reinvest in your community. Whether it be money, time, or thought, you want to get involved in the community by going to meetings, organizing activities, voting, or writing a letter to the editor.

It's good business sense to establish a relationship with your local community. You can do this by providing support for charities, leadership for a cause, or just taking part in community events. Companies that are responsible and helpful in the community will often be chosen for a job or awarded a contract.

How to Write a Commercial Job Proposal

Rather than waiting for contracts to come to you, consider identifying clients that need your services and write them a job proposal. When you seek out clients, you can target a specific area within your town or industry. Your job proposal should reflect that you've done your research on your targeted client.

The first paragraph should state the purpose of the job proposal. Introduce your business and provide a brief overview of your experience.

The second paragraph should provide more information about your cleaning business. If you are a one-person company, say so. If you have a team of people who work for you, tell a little about them. Discuss your insurance, licensing, and bonding, so your potential client doesn't have any liability concerns.

Next, explain the cleaning services you provide. Make sure this is specific to your client. If you can collect information on square footage and types of rooms beforehand, include this in the section. Discuss how you plan to clean each space and completely break down all the services you offer.

Establish a clear schedule for the janitorial services you are offering. You can propose daily or weekly cleaning. Explain the times you are available, since some clients may want you to work at night. When you have a flexible schedule, make them aware of this since this might entice the potential client.

Show your pricing information. Most clients make their decision off of the price. As we discussed before, there are a few ways in which you can price a job. Choose the best option for the job and explain it clearly in the proposal.

Lastly, you need a call to action. Provide contact information so that potential clients can get in touch with you with any questions about what you are offering. Have a contract ready that lists your price along with the janitorial services that you are going to provide. Tell your potential client that you have a contract ready or offer to email them a sample contract so they can review it before signing. This may prompt them to sign with you.

6 Factors to Include in a Commercial Contract

A commercial cleaning contract is a legally binding document. This means you are legally responsible or liable if you fail to meet the responsibilities outlined in the contract. So carefully consider each contract you sign in order to make sure you will be able to meet all the terms outlined in the contract. There are a few important elements that need to be included in any commercial cleaning contract:

1. The names of both parties should be clearly written, along with addresses and other pertinent contact information.

2. The date of the agreement, along with the term of the contract (specified down to date, month, and year).

3. Rules of termination need to be clear. For example, the nullifying party needs to provide written notice, or the contract can be terminated within 10 days of signing.

4. List and detail all cleaning responsibilities. This includes everything from the frequency of cleaning, the amount of time cleaning, and specific cleaning services to be completed.

5. Be clear on who is supplying the cleaning equipment for the performance of the above-listed services.

6. Outline procedures for what will be done if any damage or breakage occurs. Detail the steps that will be taken if there is a late or non-payment on behalf of the client.

It is always best to review any legal business documents with a lawyer. They will make sure all of the proper components are in place and that the contract fully protects both you and your business.

7 Contract Terms and Clauses You Should Know

You should be concerned with contract terms, clauses, and specifications since they are legally binding documents that outline the terms of agreement and service between you, the service provider, and the customer. For you, it is best to write and provide a service agreement and specifications to prospective customers. The contract, agreement, and specifications should be proportionate in length and detail to the account.

Any search engine can give you basic agreement and specification templates for cleaning a variety of building types and sizes. If you are dealing with an expensive account, you should have an attorney review the wording before anyone signs it.

Contracts need to be written to include any wording that a party wants to be included. There is nothing wrong with asking for changes to be made before you sign. Pay careful attention to the following clauses:

30 Days Cancellation

Most cleaning contracts will have a cancellation clause for the customer, sometimes for a cause or sometimes for no reason at all. You want to make sure you also have a way out of the agreement. You can often include this in small to medium accounts with no problem. With a larger account, it may be a little more difficult to get the customer to agree to allow you a way out of the agreement before the term is ended. A customer will likely prefer wording that allows them to cancel the contract for cause, with the cause requiring further clarification.

Start and End Date

Every contract needs a start and end date that specifies the term/length of the agreement. Normally a contract will last for a year but can be three or five-year agreements. One or more options to renew are also common. There is often a date of notice requirement that one or both parties need to comply with, specifying their intent to extend the agreement or exercise an option for an additional time period.

It isn't uncommon for companies to indefinitely renew agreements on a year to year basis. For you, the longer the renewal period, the better off you will be. Unless there are major problems, most customers don't want to change providers or go out for bids until the end of a current agreement.

Cost of Basic Supplies

You should exclude the cost of paper, soap, and plastic. These items fluctuate in price, and you don't want to take a risk if you don't have to. The best option is to either have the customer pay for the supplies you order or add a three, five, seven, or ten percent surcharge to each invoice as a handling fee.

Late Payment Penalty

Any agreement you sign should include payment terms that work well for you. This should include a late fee penalty of ten to twenty percent. Make sure you hold customers accountable if they don't pay by the due date.

These are some of the clauses you want to make sure to have included in the contract. There are also some clauses you don't want to be included. Let's consider these.

Key Loss

If you find this clause in an agreement, then you should make sure you have insurance coverage. If you have a large account, it can be tens of thousands of dollars if you have to re-key an entire building because of one lost key.

Defect Deduction

This is a clause that allows customers to deduct fees from the monthly fee based on quality control inspection defects. Make sure these clauses specify that all inspections and quality standards are done at the end of a cleaning cycle and before use. You may also want to include specific parameters for the inspection.

Labor Hours Requirement

Avoid any contract wording that gives the customer the right to examine time records or requires that you provide a specific number of labor hours.

How to Get Your First Clients

Whether you are a small or big business, you need to have a stable client base in order to grow your business and have success. Whether you clean for residential or commercial customers, getting clients that fit with your business plan requires research and commitment.

While some customers may find you, most cleaning business owners need to seek out potential customers and use marketing tactics to attract them. But first, you need to get yourself some neatly done business cards. That is the first thing you should do, and there are plenty of online and offline ways to get them done for very little cost.

Remember to come up with a catchy name and maybe a logo so both of those can describe you and your business at a glance.

How to Get Your First Residential Cleaning Clients

For residential cleaning clients, it isn't that difficult. First, you want to create a list of characteristics you are looking for in clients. Then you can focus on advertising to clients in this target market using traditional neighborhood marketing tactics such as newspapers, magazines, radio, television, or direct mail advertising if you have the budget for it. You can also hang fliers, make a few cold calls, and simply knock on doors to introduce yourself to the neighborhood.

Consider setting up referral partnerships with other cleaning businesses. They may not serve the same clients like you, but they can refer clients to you when, and you can do likewise in return. At the same time, you can talk to your current residential cleaning customers and ask for referrals to people they think would benefit from your services. You can persuade them by offering discounts for referrals or a cashback bonus if the referral results in a signed contract.

How to Get Your First Commercial Contracts

It can be a little more challenging to get your first commercial contracts. I wasted a lot of time in my ten years trying to find the best way to get commercial contracts, so hopefully, you can learn from me, and it will be easier for you.

Networking

Networking is extremely important when getting commercial cleaning contracts. However, networking isn't going to get you instant results. The focus of networking is about making relationships, and this takes time to build. When you network, you expose yourself to many other business people in the region. Once you know people, then everyone can look out for each other's interests by referring to each other. It is recommended that you join several different networking groups in order to have as many referrals as possible. This is a wonderful long term way to increase business.

Direct Mail

This is possibly the best way to find cleaning contracts in your area. You need to draft a good sales letter, about two pages. Add a flier that highlights a special offer to draw potential customers to your business. The most difficult part is writing the sales letter. This can easily lead to a number of commercial contracts. When doing direct mail out, try and see if you can remind the potential customers about a "need" like "Spring Cleaning" or any such time when people do need a cleaning service to get them started on the right track.

Via Real Estate Agents

This is a little-known tactic for getting commercial cleaning contracts. Real estate agents often need cleaning services before a house is sold or after they close. When you seek out real estate agents and ask them to refer your business, you can get a nice little niche business going.

Display Ads in Newspapers

You can create ads of different sizes that can be placed in various sections of the newspaper. You can do them in black and white or color. While this option can bring you some clients, it shouldn't be your first method.

Most people do their business and searching online; not many go to print ads anymore. Unless you know the local businesses in your area are going to be looking here, you probably don't want to waste your money on this option.

If you do decide to go this route, maybe you can try and see how humor works, as it has worked wonder for me over the years, I usually use a funny clip art like what you see below, and I have noticed how that can pique people's interest more than just using text in the ad.

Property Management Companies

Property management companies, like real estate agents, can be a good source of regular niche commercial contracts. The best way to contact these companies is through a two-page sales letter with an attached flier in a direct mail campaign.

Start by creating a list of all property management companies in the area and decide which ones you want to mail. When they contact you, set up an appointment to discuss what their needs are and go from these with bidding and signing a contract.

Phone Books

Again this is an advertising method that isn't used too much anymore. Not many businesses turn to the phone book to look for a cleaning business. Although it all comes down to the businesses in your area. If you find that you can get a decent number of contracts to recoup the cost of advertising in a phone book, then go for it.

Websites

In today's electronic society, you definitely want to have a website for your business. You can provide the whole story about your company on a website, something you don't have room for on brochures, business cards, and sales letters. You don't need to spend a lot of money on a website. In fact, there are several free services that allow you to build your own website. Just make sure you have a professional and easy to navigate website so people can contact you when they are interested in your services.

Telemarketing

For the right person, making cold calls can be a profitable option for commercial cleaning businesses. However, this only works for the right type of person. You need a calming demeanor and the ability to handle rejection.

Craigslist

This is one of the better online tools for a cleaning business. You can post to the classifieds for free and reach a wide regional audience. There is nothing at risk with this advertising method, so even if you get only one commercial contract out of it, you're coming out ahead.

As you can tell, there are many options for finding your first clients when starting a cleaning business. The important thing is to research what works best in your area and go with it. However, if you find something isn't working, then don't waste time and money sticking with it. But first find out which of these methods can get you cleaning jobs that fastest and then go from there, after all, you want to get started, so you can focus on growing your business.

6 Quickest Ways to Get Cleaning Jobs

For any cleaning business, both residential and commercial, the hardest part is getting momentum. There is a lot of competition in the cleaning business, and you really need to work on gaining the momentum to start your business. If you want to get started right away, then consider the following six ways to get cleaning jobs the quickest.

Community Networking

This isn't necessarily the same as networking that I talked about earlier. Networking and referrals can take a long time to develop. This is about making yourself well known throughout the local community. This means showing up at neighborhood meetings, going to charity functions, and shopping in local stores. When you do this, you can get to know people in your area as well as local business owners who may need your services.

Direct Mail Fliers

I talked about this above with commercial contracts, but it works for both residential and commercial. It is often the most effective way to spread the word about your company both quickly and cheaply. If you don't have the money to start out a direct mailing, then consider posting a flier on heavy traffic areas like grocery stores. If you want to go the mail route, a cheaper option can be postcards. You can always start small and work yourself up to larger direct mail campaigns as you reinvest some money back into your business marketing and advertising.

Real Estate Agents and Property Managers

I already covered these two pretty well under commercial contracts, so I won't take too much time again. However, this can certainly be a fast way to get large or multiple contracts. This gives you access to multiple types of properties so you could end up with a variety of different contracts.

Newspaper Ads

I know I said earlier that these methods of advertising are not as common. However, it is still a quick and simple way to potentially get some starting contracts. Classified ads aren't that expensive and don't take that long to put together.

Websites

As I said before, everyone needs a website. You can quickly put together a simple website to showcase what you have to offer. Consider offering a promotional discount to those who contact you through the website.

Referrals and Word of Mouth

This isn't necessarily a fast way to get contracts, but it will be the easiest, cheapest, and most effective. Talk to people about your business and make sure they pass it along to others. If you're cleaning an apartment tell them to talk to their neighbors. Often, if people are satisfied with the job you do, then they will be happy to pass your name along to others that need your services.

While there are many ways to get cleaning contracts, there are few that stand out from the rest. It is a good idea to mix a variety of options, so you get contracts quickly, but also have the opportunity to keep contracts coming in as your business grows.

How to Make Your Cleaning Company Stand Out

The best way to satisfy clients, so they recommend you to others and keep hiring you for other projects, is to stand out from the competition. When you pay attention to the small details, you will have a big impact on your clients. Consider the following simple guidelines to make your cleaning company stand out from the competition.

If you are cleaning an office building, most employees view their desk as a personal space and extension of themselves. Therefore, employees should leave a desk just as they found it, minus the dirt. The understood rule is to clean a desktop if it is clear and leave a desk that is covered with papers and projects. When cleaning, pick up with one hand while dusting with the other and put things back exactly as they originally were.

While cleaning, never set tools, cleaners, trash cans, or chairs on furniture, desks, counters or upholstery. These items can scratch surfaces, and trash cans can leak or spoil the finish off furniture.

If you move something, clean it. If you need to move furniture or a fixture, then take the time to clean all sides and the floor underneath. Also, be careful to move slowly. You don't want to move things around and cause damage carelessly.

Always point out problems and ask a client what should be done. Furniture and fixtures all need to be replaced at some point, but you shouldn't try to fix something yourself, no matter how minor.

If something gets broken or damaged, be sure to leave a note for the client. No matter how careful you are, things occasionally get broken. Make sure your employees know to report broken or damaged items.

These are just a few simple and small details, but you can see how they will have a major impact on the clients. This will make you a professional in the eyes of the clients, and they will be more likely to recommend you to others who need your services.

A Day in the Life inside the Cleaning Business

Residential and commercial cleaning follows pretty much the same cleaning process. The basics are always the same, with only a change in some specialized cleaning areas. Let's break down each room in a residential home and see what cleaning processes you should perform.

Dusting

The first step upon entering a property is to dust. The focus is to dust from the top down so you can vacuum up any dust the falls on the floor. Be sure to dust all of the following areas:

- Vents
- Ceiling fans
- Window sills and ledges
- Top of door frames
- Corner to corner of ceilings
- Lamps and shades
- Blinds
- Picture frames
- Shelves
- Furniture
- Baseboards

Bathrooms

After dusting around the whole house, I like to move into the bathrooms. In the bathroom, you should do the following:

- Clean and disinfect
- Clean soap dish and containers

- Polish faucets
- Clean mirrors

Kitchen

My next stop is usually the kitchen. This includes the following:

- Clean and disinfect
- Clean outside of refrigerator, dishwasher, stove, oven, and microwave
- Wipe down cabinets
- Sweep and mop

Property

After the three main areas are done, you can now focus on the basic cleaning of the rest of the house:

- Sweep, mop, and vacuum
- Empty and change garbage cans
- Clean light switches and doorknobs

Specialty Services

If the client requests any additional services do them along with the upper cleaning process as needed:

- Clean the inside of the refrigerator
- Clean inside of the oven
- Window cleaning
- Laundry and ironing
- Change bed linens
- Degrease stovetop
- Clean inside of cabinet shelves
- Polish silver
- Sweep or mop porch and garage

- Clean fireplace
- Clean silk plants
- Clean baseboards

Commercial Cleaning

As with residential cleaning, you want to start with dusting and window cleaning. From there, I usually focus on waste removal. I spend most of my time cleaning the bathrooms, as described above, for residential cleaning. Then you can clean the kitchen or break room if there is one. Clean up the office area. Finish up with sweeping, mopping or vacuuming floors. The main specialized cleaning in a commercial building that you will have to set time aside for would be any sanitation processes.

Safety on the Job

When you own a cleaning business, safety should be your top priority. Especially in today's world, where everyone wants to file lawsuits over little things. When you are cleaning it is important, you always focus on safety first. This only requires a little planning but goes a long way towards protecting you, your employees and your business.

The first thing is to be aware of where you leave your equipment and supplies. If you leave them scattered about, you are inviting an accident to happen. If you are cleaning while the staff is present, they are going about their job and may not be aware of what is going on around them. This means you need to be aware of their safety at all times. Therefore, leave your equipment and supplies out of traffic lanes and away from blind corners.

Second, make sure vacuum cords and extension cords are a bright color so everyone can clearly see them. If possible, don't string cords across an aisle or over a partition. While you may think bright yellow or orange cords are easily seen, most people still don't pay attention to them. You can be extra safe by placing a wet floor sign over the cord, so people take notice of it.

This brings us to the fact that you should always use wet floor signs and make sure you have enough to cover all your work areas. Place them on any floor surfaces you mop, even if you think the building is empty. You may not know if someone is working late or if someone is returning because they forgot something.

Another way to prevent slip and fall incidents is to leave a light on in the room you mopped until the floors are completely dry as it will help people see your wet floor sign. Once you are finished cleaning, return all supplies to their proper location. You don't know what happens when you are gone, and you don't want someone to spill or misuse a chemical.

When it comes to safety in the workplace, you need to think of all possible scenarios. Educate yourself on what OSHA expects of you. These are just a few of the safety issues you need to be aware of when cleaning. However, you also have to take your employees into consideration. What are some areas where they need protection?

Top 10 Concerns for You and Your Employees

As a business owner, you are constantly focusing on the safety of not only your clients but your employees as well. While providing employees with cleaning procedures, adequate training, and proper equipment and tools can go a long way to ensuring their safety, there are still some issues you may not be aware of when it comes to maintaining employee safety. Let's look at ten areas that were identified as safety concerns among cleaning business employees.

1. Blood Borne Pathogens

OSHA has a Blood Borne Pathogen Standard that was developed as a means to make cleaning and facility managers aware of the potential risks involved in blood and human waste cleanup. In certain jobs, this is obviously a big concern, but in other jobs, it may not seem like a big deal. However, when I took the time to think about it, I realized this could actually be a big area of concern. How many cleaners still clean the restrooms without wearing gloves or other protective equipment? Does your company have a policy on cleaning up potentially hazardous spills?

2. Ergonomics

Back injuries are one of the most common in the cleaning business, so you should make sure you routinely go over proper lifting methods with your employees. Every year, new cleaning tools and products are coming out that can reduce back strains or pulls: water buckets that drain without lifting, trash containers that are easier to empty, mop wringers that minimize strain, etc.

Cleaning employees are also faced with carpal tunnel syndrome caused by repetitive motions. Repetitive stress injuries can happen to the wrists, arms, and elbows after doing certain cleaning methods and using some equipment on a regular basis. You can use ergonomically designed tools and equipment along with proper training to help with these injuries.

3. Hazardous Equipment

With a down economy, the pressure is on to do more cleaning with fewer workers. As a result, you need to use more efficient equipment. For example, you can use self-propelled automatic scrubbers and propane-powered floor-care equipment in order to reduce labor needs.

However, all this technology also has some adverse effects. You must safely address the storage and operation of these pieces of equipment. The goal is to save time and labor, but you also don't want to ignore any potential dangers to the operators or the public.

4. Specialty Cleaning

There are two main theories about specialty cleaning. First, there are those who feel every cleaning business should also provide generalized services because customers rather only deal with one company that does both instead of hiring two different companies. Second is the total opposite of the first theory; in this case, specialty cleaning business owners avoid being generalized cleaners and emphasize specialty cleaning in order to attract clients and improve their overall expertise.

A lot of specialty cleaning is dangerous or hazardous work. At the very least, it is more involved and difficult. Managers pay more attention to this area because you don't want to skimp on the services offered, but you also want to make sure all safety precautions are followed.

5. Professionalism

The cleaning business goes to great lengths to provide a professional image. However, the wage gap continues to widen between unskilled cleaners and trained employees. Customers want a cleaning professional, but they also want cheap services. That is why a lot of cleaning businesses focus more on their services and less on the worker's demeanor, appearance, and training. But a good cleaning business owner is one that places important and precedence on skilled, courteous, and personable employees.

6. Lead Paint

Lead paint poses many health hazards and can lead to lawsuits. Cleaning employees don't need to be experts in lead paint removal, but managers and business owners should determine what lead hazards are present in a workplace. A dry dusting of lead-based paint is a way to create health hazards. Never allow employees to remodel or paint over lead paint surfaces unless proper safety procedures are implemented.

7. Asbestos

Asbestos dust is a carcinogenic hazard. Immediate attention and notifications are required of anyone exposed to it. Cleaning employees working around asbestos need to take all precautions to protect themselves while cleaning. But remember dealing with toxic substances such as asbestos often calls for special training, skills, protective gear, and practice. So my advice is to stay away from anything and everything that is hazardous or toxic.

8. Integrated Pest Management

Integrated Pest Management (IPM) is focused on reducing the use of toxic sprays and chemicals while still maintaining effective pest control. Employees are an important part of these programs because they are often asked to eliminate the pest problem.

9. Hazardous Chemicals

Training employees in the use of potentially hazardous cleaning chemicals can help reduce the risk of injuries and ensure the correct products are used properly. Don't settle for employees that have poor training attendance. A failure to train in this area increases liability.

10. Sick Building Syndrome

Sick building syndrome is when complaints from customers and tenants add up about dust, odors, pests, poor ventilation, irritating cleaning chemicals, allergic reactions, and faulty cleaning methods. The key is to be more experienced in analyzing complaints and provide adequate training in critical cleaning areas where diseases or chemical reactions can spread.

How to Effectively Run & Grow Your Cleaning Business

Running a successful cleaning business means you keep customers' facilities clean without affecting their day-to-day operations. If you have a lack of complaints or problems, then you are running your business well.

There are many factors that go into running a cleaning business, including scheduling and coordinating cleaning activities while also keeping sufficient staff on hand during regular business hours to handle any unforeseen events.

You should schedule your employees to clean individual workspaces and common areas on a regular basis, about twice a week or so. Keep track of how long it takes on average to clean each area and schedule additional time for places that regularly require extra attention. Get to know your employees and pay attention to what types of work they are best suited for; incorporate these observations into your scheduling

When it comes to ordering and stocking cleaning supplies, you need to keep track of how much your staff uses and develop a set schedule for ordering them. Order your products in bulk and regularly check inventory, so you know when it is time to reorder.

Either you or a designated employee should be in charge of safety issues. This should be maintaining of SDS sheets and proper maintenance of janitorial equipment.

Check-in regularly with your clients to make sure their needs are being met. Be aware of any special events a client has coming up that may require additional cleaning and, therefore, the scheduling of additional time.

13 Ways to Make Your Cleaning Business a Success

Nothing will teach you more than experience. However, if you are just getting started, let me tell you thirteen ways I've learned from ten years of experience that can help make your business a success.

1. Always Learn New Things

The cleaning industry is neither glamorous nor complex, but as any cleaning business owner can tell you, there is always something to learn. Technology is always improving the equipment you use; safety issues are always affecting the chemicals you use, and there is always a way to improve your organizational and managerial skills. Take the time to read industry publications, go to meetings and conventions, participate in trade organizations and stay up to date.

2. Use Your Resources

There are a number of associations that serve all aspects of the professional cleaning industry. You can use these groups as a way to help with operational, marketing and management issues. For small businesses, you can also get help from many state and government agencies.

3. Treat It Like Your Own Home

Whether you are cleaning a home or a large office, always clean as if you were cleaning your own home. This will help you to go the extra mile and provide professional service to your clients.

4. Have a System

As you expand and start hiring employees, you are going to need a way to provide consistency and efficiency. Systems help provide this structure and allow the company to continue running even if you're not there. Have a system in place for all the functions of your business: cleaning, laundry, supervision, reporting, customer service, accounting, and management.

5. Use Caution

While time is money in the cleaning business, you also don't want to rush to the point that you get careless. Customers understand that accidents will happen, but you don't want to rely on this. Also, the cost to repair something can quickly add up, so it's more cost-effective if you take more time and work carefully.

6. Don't Undersell

When you first start your business, you may be tempted to undercut the competition's prices in order to get a job. A better strategy is to outperform them and gain a reputation that allows clients to hire you even if you cost a little more.

7. Take Care of Employees

As you grow, employees become critical to your business success. An employee's performance quality is what determines if your customers are satisfied or not. Look for ways to get your employees to perform their best. Train employees well and don't micromanage. Treat all employees with respect and listen to them. Provide bonuses and incentives for top performance and consider offering perks.

8. Create a Niche

Don't try to be all-encompassing. Rather pick a market that you can best serve and focus on it. Excel in one area and build consistency in the services you provide. If you try to serve too many markets, you will have a hard time being successful in just one.

9. Focus on Computer Skills

Cleaning may not seem like a computer-based business, but in today's world of technology, you need computer skills. You will need to do estimates, billing, payroll, inventory control, and other record-keeping; these can be done by hand, but you'll save a lot of time and effort by doing it on the computer.

10. Keep Track of Labor Costs

The biggest expense in your cleaning business is labor, and you need to keep track of it. If you aren't watching labor costs on a daily basis, then they will get away from you. Compile a daily over and under report so you can easily spot trends before they develop into a major issue. If your labor is increasing, then determine where the problem is and fix it. Are customers asking for extra services that aren't getting charged for? Was the time to complete a job underestimated?

11. Focus on Customer Service

The quality of cleaning is important, but it isn't everything. You also want to develop a strong relationship with your clients through a serious commitment to customer service. Don't assume that just because a cleaning job looks good to you that your customers are completely satisfied. Always follow up with clients to see how things are going.

12. Watch the Economy

There will always be a need for professional cleaners, but economic changes can impact your market. For example, residential cleaning is often seen as a luxury when there is an economic downturn. When business profits shrink, they will often look for ways to cut expenses, which means reducing or eliminating services such as cleaning.

The economy can also impact the cost of running your business. If oil prices climb, it costs more to operate your vehicles. As the cost of lumber goes up, so do basic paper supplies. While you may be able to pass along some of these costs, don't rely on them to keep your business profitable. Have a plan in place in case you need to shift your market focus to stay afloat.

13. Be Selective

You don't have to take every job that comes along; you don't want to accept a job that doesn't make money. You should also turn down any work that is undesirable. Focus your time and energy on profitable work that you enjoy.

4 Creative Ways to Win Major Accounts

As you grow and expand your business, you are going to want to focus on larger cleaning accounts. These big accounts rely more on your attitude and management rather than cleaning ability. The focus of commercial cleaning is getting a larger account that can provide sustainable capital. There is a lot of hard work that goes into this phase of business growth, but there are few things that can help you win these major accounts.

Know Your Target Market

High-pressure sales tactics don't work for larger accounts. These clients know what they want and what they don't need. No one is going to convince them otherwise.

Don't push and oversell when it comes to large accounts unless you understand the true need of the client. They want you to fix their problem, not shower them with colorful brochures and mailing. Know your client, the types of issues they are facing, and outline a clear plan to accomplish their goals.

Fulfill a Need

Know how to price for the job you are going to propose. Larger clients aren't necessarily looking for the lowest bidder. Rather these clients simply want someone that can take something off their plate.

If you fill the need they are looking for, then they will stick with you and avoid the time it takes to change vendors. Filling a need is the best way to maintain a relationship with both large and small clients.

Have Initiative

Show your clients that you are willing and able to do things that may not be your responsibility. These clients like a vendor who can take ownership of situations that come up and deal with problems with minimal interruption to their day-to-day business operations.

Be Properly Equipped

Be sure you have the proper equipment and staff to stand behind what you are proposing to do. If you don't, then these clients will know that, and it won't look too professional on your part.

Top 10 Tips to Close the Sale

Once you are starting bidding on contracts and attracting the large accounts, you will need to be able to sell yourself and close the sale. In order to effectively sell yourself and close the deal, you need to see things from the customers' perspective. There are ten things you want to focus on when closing a sale.

1. **Quality** - No matter what the price, customers want good service, so they don't have to deal with issues. Sell your quality service of cleaning and maintenance.

2. **Professionalism** - You need to look and sound the part. A large account customer isn't

looking for a friend; they want a serious business relationship.

3. **Guarantees** - You need to stand behind what you and your staff do. Make sure your customer is aware that should a problem arise, you will make it right.

4. **References** - Mention and provide a list of current or previous clients who will provide a good word about your services. You can also reassure prospective customers by showing photos of buildings with details that prove you can handle their needs.

5. **Trained Staff** - Have a short bio and photo for all staff ready. Make sure the bio clearly lists all of their special skills, training, and time they have been on staff with you. This will reassure the customer that you hire only qualified staff and management to get the job done right.

6. **Local Business** - Stress the fact that you are a local small business owner who specializes in serving the community and other local business owners. You can even mention your involvement in any local organizations or events.

7. **Specialized** - Talk about any specialties you offer for certain types, sizes, and locations if it applies to the account you are trying to close.

8. **Competitive Pricing** - In a local marketplace, you have to be competitive. You probably won't get the job if you are the highest price unless no one else is bidding. However, you don't want to go the lowest. When you know your costs and bid, competitively you will still be able to make money on the account.

9. **Other Accounts** - Let a customer know if you have other accounts nearby. This means you

always have staff in the area to handle any special needs that may arise.

    10. **Personal Attention** - Assure the customer that their business is very important to you and that you will give their needs your personal attention throughout the life of the account.

You need to be able to close a sale without overselling it. Don't do all the talking. Allow the customer time to talk while you listen attentively. Be sure to ask relevant questions to show you are interested and dedicated to the customer. When you do this, you will be able to close the deal on all accounts, both large and small.

How to Hire and Train the Right Employees

One of the biggest issues in the cleaning business is employee turnover. This is why a lot of corporations and businesses choose to outsource in order to get rid of this problem. So basically, you are getting big accounts because of the biggest challenge you face when starting a new cleaning business.

While the general skills needed to do cleaning work means you have a wide pool of potential employees, the turnover can be as high as 200 to 300 percent a year. No one wants to make a career out of cleaning. Therefore, your best chance to get people to stay longer is to pay above minimum wage and train your employees for advancement within the company. Another option is to hire part-time personnel or transients like students who can work flexible and irregular hours.

What is Effective Training

Training is going to be most effective when you use it as a tool for supervision and management. Training isn't effective if it is done on a set schedule or only done as a way to solve a problem or correct behaviors. Training needs to be a mindset that guides you on approaching and interacting with the staff, customers, and others whose behavior you want to influence.

In order for you to have long-term success with training, it needs to be ongoing and reinforced with follow-up refresher courses that keep the information easily accessible in mind. Training should start before an employee is even hired and then continue indefinitely with each interaction you have with individuals.

Why Train

When it comes to conveying information and skills, the best and most realistic option a supervisor, manager, or business owner has is training. Employees need training in order to perform their assigned tasks correctly. Threatening and intimidating your employees are never a positive solution and the end results are often destructive. So again, training is the best and most realistic option when it comes to having an influence on their positive behaviors.

Identifying Core Training Needs

The first place to look for training needs is to ask your workers if there are any subjects they want to know more about or that would benefit them on the job.

Another option is to survey building occupants and see how they view the level of service they get from your company. A lot of managers are nervous about this since they don't want to get a list of complaints or problems. However, if you don't encourage feedback, you won't know what you need to do to improve. If people have a problem with your company, it would be better that you hear them than other prospective clients.

Lastly, how does a completed job look to you? Do you think a better job could have been done? What are the complaints or requests you've received within the last thirty to sixty days? Is there a pattern of customer complaints that indicate some aspect of work that could be improved with some training?

If you still can't come up with anything after going over the above three areas, then there are some stand-by subjects that you should repeat every six months or so:

- Restroom cleaning
- Office cleaning
- Safety and health
- Care of equipment and supplies
- Company policy reviews
- Team cleaning
- Bloodborne pathogen precautions
- Indoor environmental quality
- Repetitive stress injury prevention

You can also choose to go with some training topics that are non-work-related, but still provide valuable information:

- Human relations and communications
- English as a second language
- Remedial reading, writing, and arithmetic
- Personal growth and investment strategies

Training Methodology

When it comes to how you are going to present or conduct training, you have many options. These can range from classroom presentations to guest speakers to videotapes and written handouts or training manuals.

A newer option is an interactive computer-based training program. These programs operate on a computer, come on a CD and incorporate video clips, audio and allow the participant to interact in a number of ways. These types of training programs also track an individual's progress so management can monitor it and evaluate each training session.

In order for training to be effective, it needs to be ongoing and not something that is only done when a worker is new to the job. For maximum impact, all training programs should include classroom presentations, on the job training, and one to one discussions between workers and supervisors.

Classrooms, videos, and computers are great for presenting information, but if you want to improve performance, then nothing is better than ten or fifteen minutes of video training, then having a discussion about what they saw on the video.

However, the drawback is that this type of training takes up a lot of time, is sometimes uncomfortable for both parties, and isn't as easy as simply talking about what needs to be done. However, this method of training is effective in solving and preventing problems, reducing complaints, improving performance and developing a better relationship between workers.

Although time-consuming, spending fifteen minutes with each worker once a month with hands-on training is a great investment of your time. People learn best by doing and from personal interaction, not by talking about what they need to do.

However, keep in mind that you are dealing with a wide variety of people who come from different backgrounds with a range of interests and abilities. Therefore, you need to keep an open mind on the best ways to absorb and comprehend information. There isn't a one size fits all when it comes to employee training. So don't expect the results to be the same across the board. Keep in mind that training is an on-going process, and it takes time to get desired results.

Interactive Learning

This form of interactive learning is highly effective and valuable. The main reason is that it prevents attendees from mentally leaving the room or doing something else such as texting. When learners are thinking, talking, reading, writing or physically interacting then it is difficult for them to do anything else. Active participation in a training session means a high percentage of learners stay mentally engaged.

The goal of the instructor is to facilitate a learning experience for participants and keep the mind fully engaged. For instructors, this can be a challenge. In fact, it is much easier to talk or lecture or show a video than it is to plan and execute interactive learning. The problem with lectures is that it bores attendees and allows the mind to wander off, and then the learning stops.

The biggest challenge with interactive learning is that the instructor needs to take a lot of time and effort to plan and execute the instruction. However, this extra effort is worth it, and after a little practice, you will get used to it.

What Goes Into Interactive Learning

With interactive learning, you need to use different instructional techniques. This can include hands-on exercises, demonstrations, printed materials, exams, games, powerpoint, video, photos, props, handouts, question and answer sessions, group and team exercises, and limited lectures or talks. There is basically an endless list of options for you.

The main constant in interactive learning is that you break up the learning into a few ten to fifteen-minute sessions, plan in variety with as little reliance on the lecture as possible. When planning interactive learning, think less about what you will say and more about what you are going to have the learner doing during the training session.

Goals of Interactive Training

Interactive training isn't focused on the information you convey or how you present it; rather, the focus and goal is getting the learner to retain and use the information and skills they are being taught. The truest test of interactive teaching is whether or not the information and skills are used.

A good instructor will help the learner understand the value and importance of using their new information and skills. The best way to do this is to help them understand the personal benefits they receive from using the information or skills.

Making It Stick

For long-term success, you need to refresh the training on a regular basis. If you don't refresh it, then the information or skills learned will be filed away as unimportant and eventually forgotten. One way to do this is to use the 2, 2, 2 follow-up process.

Two days after the initial instructions, discuss the key points of what should be remembered and why it is important to use the information or skill. Try to focus on personal benefits and not just company benefits.

Two weeks after the initial instruction, again discuss the key points and then ask the learner to tell you some of the information or key points they learned about the subject and why it is important to use the information or skill on the job. Ask how it has been useful since the training.

Two months after the initial training, again discuss and ask the learner to give some examples of how they used and benefited from the information or skill they learned in the training session.

While this takes a lot of time on your part, this is what needs to be done for the training to stick and be used by employees. The learner needs to understand and recall the importance and value of the information or skills they learned. If you don't take the extra time and effort to do this, then you will be wasting your time and effort on training.

Maintain Perspective

When it comes to training, don't expect to see results overnight. Training is an investment that pays off if you develop a structured plan based on the needs of your employees, customers, and business.

Start by using the information learned to develop a one-year training outline. Next, establish the subject matters and dates for training as well as who will do the training. If you have workers or supervisors who do well in a certain area or task, then get them involved in the training process.

Keep accurate records on those who complete a segment of training and don't let those who are shy or need training slip through the cracks. At the end of the year, consider having a potluck lunch or a pizza party and present a signed certificate of completion for those who completed all aspects of the training program. You should also place a copy of the certificate in the employee's personnel record.

Top 10 Training Tips

1. Develop training as a way to supervise.
2. Start training each new employee from the first contact and don't stop.
3. Have regular training sessions, no longer than thirty minutes.

4. Stress hands-on practice rather than talking or written materials. Observe work to make sure actual learning is happening.

5. A training session should be done every 30 days, record attendance with a sign-in sheet, and prepare a written agenda for the meeting.

6. Each meeting should include safety, cleaning procedures, health, and employee issues.

7. Use visuals such as handouts, equipment, supplies, slides, videos, and guest speakers.

8. Encourage employee involvement and participation.

9. Develop and utilize written procedures for the training process.

10. Tests, evaluations, and reviews should be based on an individual's ability to perform assigned tasks in a manner that gets desired results rather than on a person's ability to remember and recite materials.

Promoting from Within: Worker to Supervisor

Due to the high turnover rate, the biggest challenge in the cleaning business is finding and keeping qualified employees. This makes the task of finding and keeping qualified supervisors and managers even more difficult. Often the best place to find new supervisors and managers is to develop and promote an individual from within the company.

If an employee consistently does a good job, shows up on time, then be inclined to offer them a responsible position. This helps provide opportunities for advancement in your company.

However, in order for this to be successful, you need to prepare the individuals for the responsibilities of the new position and help them with the transition from worker to supervisor.

Speaking from experience, when I first started running my business after being the sole worker, there are two main problems new supervisors face. The first is the duties of a supervisor or manager, and the second is the mental transition from worker to supervisor. This mental transition is often why people fail when they are promoted to a management position.

For those who are interested in a management position or those showing potential for upward mobility, a pre-lead training program will improve the success rate and make the process less stressful. Let's consider some of the topics that should be taught in a pre-lead training program.

There will be a change of relationships on the job, and these need to be dealt with. For some employees, the new manager will be going from coworker to enemy overnight. A new manager needs to learn how to separate friendship and job responsibilities based on their new role and position in the company.

It is important to train on words and conversations. It is important to focus on what and how you say things. Learn to control responses to questions, actions, and comments since what you say carries weight and can be twisted or misinterpreted. Sometimes the wrong words or actions can reinforce wrong thoughts or behaviors.

Teach when to be silent. Every day supervisors and managers are privy to personal and business data that is often confidential in nature. You need to control your desire to talk about things you know, but shouldn't be repeated or discussed with those who aren't a member of the management team.

When others are openly discussing a subject, supervisors and managers can't be free to make comments or give opinions or thoughts on issues. When you speak as a supervisor or manager, then others hear you as speaking for the company. The best approach is to learn to keep your thoughts and comments to yourself.

Get the new supervisor or manager immersed in the organization. Involve them in meetings; give them projects and assignments that expose them to the higher positions within the business.

How to accept responsibility for their own mistakes, rather than defending themselves, teach them how they can instead learn from their mistakes as a part of growth and self-improvement process.

Ways to protect health, exercise, eat right, and don't take work issues home or bring home issues to work. Learn when and how to separate work from personal and family life.

Evaluate and utilize current supervisor training programs on the market or available within your company, along with private resources.

Train on how to understand people and on how to deal effectively with all personality types.

Learn how to understand and respect internal politics and the bureaucracy of the workplace. Learn who has unofficial authority and respect within the organization.

Understand the chain of command structure and follow the business etiquette.

Encourage them to seek mentors both within and outside the business in order to talk and discuss issues.

Strengthen the ability to read and write well.

Support the willingness and courage to make prompt decisions.

How to avoid favoritism and how to deal with such issues at the first sign.

Make sure all actions are fair and within the law so that they can be defendable during claims of discrimination. Make sure they are aware that what they do and say can have legal ramifications.

Train a thorough understanding of the importance and a willingness to follow all business policies, procedures, and processes along with the related documentation.

Focus training on the number one factor of safety. There is no allowance for working in an unsafe environment or committing unsafe acts.

Teach computer, internet, and social media skills to help increase the outreach of your business.

They possess a willingness to learn and are not afraid to make mistakes.

Developing a Pre-Lead Training Program

A pre-lead training program needs to use interactive training and be phased in over time with a multistep process that uses a blend of learning styles, including role-playing, presentations, self-study, shadowing, mentoring, and hands-on involvement in all departments and business operations.

Some of the difficulties in pre-lead training programs that you will be faced with include time, money, turnover, resistance to change, fear, and self-doubt. However, if you can encourage a trainee to stay and learn from their mistakes, then the program will be successful.

Monitoring Your Business and Dealing with Issues

Knowing exactly what customers and potential future customers are looking for in a cleaning business is important. This can help you stay focused on what areas of your business to maintain high standards while also being prepared for where customer issues might come from.

What Customers Want

Consider some of the most important things that customers want from a cleaning business.

1. **Commitment to Quality** - If you aren't offering quality products, you can't expect to get the attention of clients.

2. **Cost Competitive** - Competitive pricing is big among clients. However, clients are willing to pay more if products and/or services are of exceptionally high quality or green products or procedures are used.

3. **Communication** - Customers want a cleaning business that can be reached quickly and responds promptly. No one wants to be faced with an issue and has trouble reaching the business they hired.

4. **Access to Knowledge** - Clients don't know what products are most effective, and they only want results. They want to hire a company that has access to knowledge on all products based on effectiveness and environmental considerations.

5. **Perks** - Clients like getting extra perks, whether it is a cleaning business available after-hours or the occasional discount.

6. **Reliable Delivery** - This is high on the client's lists. They want a cleaning business that is reliable and consistent. It is also good when a business is available at all hours to work within the client's schedule.

Warning Signs of Difficult Clients

Clients are everything in the cleaning business. There are the clients that you enjoy because it doesn't take much to please them, and you don't have to go out of your way to please them. On the other hand, we dread having to deal with those clients that whine and complain in hopes of getting their way or paying less.

How can you spot these difficult clients, and what should you do about them?

You will often be able to notice the warning signs of a difficult client even before you start working for them. The biggest clue is the individuals who only want a phone quote. These are the price shoppers that want the cheapest option available. You don't want to target these accounts because these clients aren't likely to value what they can get from a reputable cleaning service; they are only concerned about the price.

If you are faced with these individuals, don't negotiate or low-ball your offer because you aren't likely to make a profit. If you take on these accounts, your quality level will drop because you will be trying to accomplish it sooner in order to get a profit. This poor level of service will then affect your reputation in the cleaning marketplace.

Another warning sign of a difficult client is those who have contracted with multiple other cleaning businesses before. If a prospective client reveals that they have used other cleaning services before, find out the reason they switched. They could be like the price shopper, or they could just be a highly picky customer who is never satisfied no matter who is doing their cleaning. You want to know who canceled the contract and what the reason was. Once you gather all the facts, you will know whether or not you should take on these accounts.

There are also some signs to look for once you have an agreement and start cleaning. These are the clients that are never satisfied with anything. They may have the cleanest house, but they still aren't satisfied. Clients who are always complaining require a lot of time and energy, so identifying them early and "firing" them is important. The longer you take to recognize them, the more difficult it will be to get rid of them.

Then there are the clients who want something different done each time you go to clean. These are also difficult clients to have since the cleaning business relies on systems and repetitiveness. Constant special requests hinder your cleaning efforts, causing an increase in labor hours and a decrease in profits.

Another warning sign is customers who pay late. If clients pay late early in the contract, then this is likely to continue. Can you deal with the late payments? Cash flow is often an issue for cleaning businesses since this business is much labor-intensive. Whether a client pays or not, you still need to make payroll and meet other expenses. If you can cover costs while waiting for payment and the client is otherwise easy to deal with, you may choose to keep the account.

You should also be aware of a client that puts down their previous cleaning service. There are obviously good reasons to fire a cleaning service and hire another, but a client who keeps talking bad about their old service should be a red flag. If they choose to let you go sometime in the future, then they will do the same to you. This will give you a bad reputation, and that can be difficult to overcome in the cleaning business.

Learn to identify these red flags and realize that it may be necessary to turn down new prospective clients or "fire" existing clients if they aren't worth the effort to keep them. If it takes too much time and energy for a contract, then don't keep them.

Although you may also have a good client that has a legitimate complaint. Next, let's look at the most common complaints from clients and how you can deal with them.

Top Cleaning Complaints

A recent survey of the complaints received by cleaning businesses identified the following top cleaning complaints:

- Dusting

- Restrooms/bathroom
- Vacuuming
- Mopping
- Trash
- Restroom supplies
- Door glass/windows
- Broken items
- Detail cleaning
- Other
- Doors unlocked
- Employee turnover

Now that we know what some of the top complaints are among cleaning businesses, let's take a look at five ways you can reduce these complaints.

Customer complaints are inevitable in the cleaning business, but there are several things you can do to reduce their frequency. Let's look at some of the common complaints and get some tips on how to solve them.

5 Ways to Solve Common Cleaning Complaints

Dusting

Inadequate dusting is the most common complaint by far. This is because the crew is in a rush and will often neglect to dust first. This is because it is less noticeable than not emptying a garbage can. Microfiber cloths or dusters are a good way to help with this. These will pick up dust rather than move it around or make it airborne, which means it won't resettle onto surfaces.

Also make sure your employees pay attention to commonly missed areas such as build-up around calculators, stacking baskets, pictures, sides of desks, and chair legs. Lastly, make sure your supervisors and managers pay extra attention to this area when they do their walkthrough of the building.

Restrooms/Bathrooms

This is the second most common area of complaint. Restroom training programs should lay out each step for cleaning a restroom. Since there are often a lot of steps involved in cleaning a restroom, it is easy for a new employee to forget an important step, and this can lead to a complaint.

One simple solution is to use color-coded microfiber cloths. For example, use a blue cloth for cleaning mirrors and polished stainless steel, a red cloth for toilets and urinals, and a yellow cloth for countertops, sinks, dispensers, partitions, and walls.

A common complaint about restrooms has to do with the odors coming from the floor drain. While this doesn't have anything to do with the cleaning aspect of the bathroom, it can be a good idea to take care of it. These odors are often a result of the drain drying out, so simply pouring water down the drain once a week will eliminate the odor.

Vacuuming

Vacuuming is the third area of complaint. Employees should be trained to move through an office counter-clockwise in order to ensure all areas are vacuumed. If there is a mat, it should be rolled up so the area underneath can be vacuumed.

You also want to make sure your employees are using the right vacuum for the job. For example, a wide track vacuum cleaner used in tight areas such as under a desk is unlikely to pick up bits of paper or other dirt. The right vacuum should be used for the space it is cleaning. Wide track vacuums should be used for large, open areas. Backpack vacuums are good for regular office and detail work.

Trash

Trash not getting emptied is another common complaint. Make sure new employees have a specific path to follow, so no trash can is missed, and be sure to point out hidden trash cans. Typically employees should go counter-clockwise around a room, zigzag down aisles or hallways. A good double-check is to look for garbage cans that may have been missed while vacuuming.

Supply Shortage

The biggest issue is in the bathroom. If your toilet paper or paper towel rolls aren't staying full until your next cleaning day, consider adding a bigger roll if possible. If you have to, you may need to get a bigger dispenser.

If you can't replace the dispensers, then teach employees how to properly stock dispensers. Hand towel dispensers should be filled to the brim, but rather two-thirds full. When dispensers are filled to the brim, a lot of weight is put on the bottom towels, so they end up tearing apart when being pulled out of the dispenser. If you need, you can consider a second dispenser or simply leaving an extra stack on the counter. The same applies to toilet paper.

These are just five of the more common areas. When you consistently train employees with detailed training programs, you can avoid all customer complaints. Perhaps once a month, you can consider the top complaints you are receiving and do a refresher training course in these areas to keep your employees aware of what is going on and keep your clients satisfied.

How to Effectively Deal with Difficult Clients

Even with all the work you do on recognizing and avoiding red flag clients and keeping on top of common complaints, you are still going to have to deal with difficult customers at some point. In order to calm tempers, diffuse conflict and solve complaints quickly with good results, you need to handle the customer and not the complaint.

Having happy and satisfied customers is the basis for any cleaning business; they are the sustainability and growth of a company. Growth and profit benefit from a strong, positive reputation based on customer satisfaction and repeat business.

Unhappy customers often fit into two different groups: those who are upset and those who are difficult. If a reasonable person gets upset, they may momentarily lose reasonableness, but they are still basically rational. On the other hand, difficult people have a psychological need to get attention by being disruptive and negative. These individuals are hard to communicate with and are usually never satisfied.

Some of the techniques you use to calm an upset customer will also work for difficult individuals. However, for difficult clients, you often have to reach deep into your people skill strategies, and you may still find the only resolution is to terminate the relationship. The key is to identify which type of client you are dealing with and then determine if they are worth your continued efforts or if you should get rid of them.

Let's look at the more common upset customer, the ones who likely have a legitimate complaint about services received through your company. You want to encourage your customers to tell you if something is not right with the service they receive. If you don't know about a problem, you can't fix it. You never want to find out about a problem through social media or online reviews.

When you stay calm and resolve the issue in an amicable way, you will be able to have a continued relationship and build a positive reputation. This is especially true when a company is at fault. No one wants to be on the receiving end of an irate client, but your response is what will determine the outcome. Consider the following six tips to have success in dealing with these customers.

1. Attitude is projected through tone of voice. Your voice should be friendly and helpful. People are more likely to respond to how you say something rather than what you say.

2. Get all the facts from the customer's point of view. Ask the customer to tell you in detail about what happened.

3. Words can make all the difference. When you use words that create a defensive reaction, it can escalate the negative situation. Don't use words that start an argument.

4. Use words to calm the customer. If you use calming words, you will change the direction of the situation immediately.

5. Never ask a customer to call back. Rather you should be the one to initiate the return call.

6. Try to handle complaint issues through the phone when possible. Electronic communication takes out the personal factor and is important in customer satisfaction.

You never want to make employees look incompetent, but as a business owner, you need to take ownership of a problem. You should revisit training and follow-up procedures in order to get a swift resolution that will satisfy the customer. This is a part of handling the customer and not the complaint.

If a complaint is repeated for the same cleaning team, employee, or task, then you should investigate the process you have in place. If the complaint is about staff, then you should review the training and follow-up process to see where improvements can be made.

Customer satisfaction is the key to your cleaning business's success and survival. Customers know when you care about them and will seek out companies that can demonstrate this care and concern. You want your company to be one of them.

5 Ways to Getting Out of a Bad Contract

Even after all the work you put into fixing complaints and working with difficult clients, things may still not work out for you. Perhaps things looked good when you bid on a job; everything went well at first, but then after a few days, weeks, or months, you find out for some reason or another that you are spending too much money on an account and not making a profit.

There are several causes for this failure to bid appropriately. You missed something, didn't ask the right questions, overlooked a detail or two of specifications, didn't realize how difficult a customer was going to be, made an error in your calculations, or the client gave you incorrect information. This can happen for both one-time services and as a result of changes that take place on an account due to more staff, overtime, construction, weather, or high demands from the client.

No matter what the reason, the point is that you are losing money on the account. The question is not only why it's happening, but what you can do about it. There are several options to consider.

Deal with It

You can simply stick with the account. Learn from your mistake, and don't do it again. This is often easy to do if you are dealing with a small or short-term financial loss. However, if it is a bigger contract and a lot of money is at stake that can potentially put you out of business, then you need to take immediate action.

Ask for More

If the problem comes from the customer giving you incorrect information, then you have good reason to explain the situation to the client and ask for additional money. This doesn't necessarily mean the client will give it to you, but you are on firm ground when asking for some adjustment to pricing.

Talk It Out

Always go to the customer and explain the situation. Then explain that you need an increase in order to provide the level of service they deserve and expect. Ask for the customer's understanding and help in finding a way to solve the problem since you can't afford to lose money on the account. A lot of customers will be happy for your honesty and will be willing to negotiate.

Adjust the Work

Perhaps you can adjust the way the work is done in order to reduce costs so you can at least break even or make a small profit. This is an internal process that doesn't need to involve the customer unless the contract obliges you to provide a set number of employees or hours. However, as long as the work is acceptable to the customer, then you should be fine.

Walk Away

This should always be your last resort option. Your reputation with the client will suffer. If you have a formal contract for specific services, there is the chance of legal threats or an actual lawsuit when you walk away from an account. The one thing you can count on is not getting work from the client again. If the client is well connected, or you live in a small community, then the word is going to spread. This means you will need to answer questions from potential customers as to why you walked away from an account.

After you have dealt with these worthless contracts, you won't want it to happen again. There are a few things you can do to prevent getting bad contracts again and lose money on future jobs.

4 Step Analysis to Identify Future Job Contracts

Watch Your Numbers

Double and triple check numbers whenever you submit a bid. You should also have someone else read your proposal and double-check all the numbers. You may be too close to spot errors, and your mind will see what you wanted to say or write even if that isn't what you actually wrote.

Compare

Compare your bid and job to other accounts you may have that are similar. Does everything make sense, and if not, what is the difference that caused the cost to go up or down on the accounts. If there is something that doesn't look right or you can't figure it out, then you should look at the details again and find out where the difference in price is happening. Look closely at labor hours since this is where the majority of costs are, but also don't overlook supply and equipment costs as well as overhead and profit.

Risks

It is riskiest to bid on large, complex contracts or work you aren't familiar with. If you aren't sure, then be sure to ask a consultant or a friendly competitor. Although if you don't know how to bed accurately for a job, then chances are you won't be qualified to do the work. Rather stick with what you know, what you are comfortable with, and grow your company slowly.

Track Everything

For every job, you should track your costs and profit. If you don't monitor, you are placing blind bids, and there is no way to build a stable and profitable business successfully. You need solid financial information in order to have a basis for your decisions and bids.

However, once you stay with a contract, you want to maintain customer satisfaction. The best way to do this is through a quality assurance program to make sure your customers are satisfied with the services you are providing.

Quality Assurance Audits

Checking up on your procedures and the results of your employees is essential to customer retention, employee training, and continual improvement of your cleaning business. Auditing for quality assurance is important and gives you information that can truly benefit your business. There are five things to include in quality assurance audits.

Why Audit?

The first step is to understand why you are auditing for quality assurance. What do you gain from quality inspections? A lot of supervisors feel they don't have time to do quality assurance inspections because they are already too busy with day-to-day operations and managing employees. However, quality assurance audits should be added as a part of your day-to-day operations because they are an important part of managing your business and employees.

At a minimum, audits allow you to measure the performance of your employees and the cleanliness of a customer's facility. While client surveys and feedback can give you the same information, it is better to find it yourself through an audit so you can fix it before your clients spot it.

Performing an audit allows you to learn where problem areas are so you can direct your valuable resources to address the most needed areas. Resources can be used for re-training, shadowing, or equipment fixes or purchases. At least you will be able to identify problems quickly and efficiently. You will also be able to note what staff does well and provide a boost in morale by acknowledging performance. As any business owner knows, the happier the staff, the more productive they are.

What and Where to Audit

This depends entirely on your cleaning business and the types of accounts you have. What is important in one facility may not be the same in another. However, at some point, you should be able to audit all areas. You should frequent the most important areas more often. Make sure you are auditing a good cross-section of room types and space in each inspection.

The items you choose to audit will also be unique, depending on the facility. Choose items of importance and those that are most likely to have problems, refer to the common list of complaints we discussed. Avoid choosing too many items in one area or attempting to do a comprehensive audit. This only leads to frustration and a loss of interest in the inspection. It is a good idea to audit about ten to fifteen items.

You also want to determine what you should be auditing. Is it visual cleanliness, environmental cleanliness, process cleaning, or all of the above. Again the answer lies in what is most important to you, the client, and the business.

When to Audit

There are a couple of forms to this question: how often and when a room is occupied or unoccupied. The question of how often is simple enough, when you can get a meaningful snapshot and trend of what is happening.

If you have a problem area, auditing once a year isn't going to be very helpful. Audit once to get a one-time snapshot of the area, but keep in mind this isn't going to tell you what is happening in the area over a period of time.

If you audit only once in a long period of time, then you may do it on a good day or a bad day, but you won't get the whole picture. Therefore, trending over a period of time is important. With trending, you can have a greater deal of certainty and consistency about what is really happening.

This type of information will give you insight into where you need to spend most of your time and focus. So when it comes to the frequency, the answer is often enough to trend appropriately.

When it comes to the when or time of day, this is again a situational choice. There are pros and cons to both sides. It is easier to move around and inspect when a space is unoccupied.

This is often less intrusive, and you can be sure you are inspecting a fully clean space rather than a partially clean space. On the other hand, some clients will want to know that you are performing regular audits, and when you are visibly seen doing so, this will impress the clients.

Who Is Auditing

Some clients prefer third party audits since they want an impartial opinion. However, audits are expensive to perform with any frequency over once a year. Then there is the matter that a third party audit often doesn't get you results for a week or two. This means you are often reacting and not being proactive. When you have your own auditing time on a regular basis, you can focus on what is most important, quality.

When your supervisors do the auditing, they get a sense of responsibility and ownership. They know their direct reports are performing. This can also help supervisors be aware of where problems are and how they can fix them.

How to Audit

What are the tools and methodologies of auditing? Many cleaning companies are getting away from paper audits. This saves on paper, time, and accuracy.

The technology combines these three functions, so electronic is the best way to go. You can do inspections on a mobile device and get critical information in real time.

You can generate reports directly from the device and share them with employees, clients, and superiors right away so that problems can be dealt with immediately.

Once reports are compiled, they can be view by employee, facility, or area type. You can view results for a week, month, or quarter. This allows you to choose the methodology you want to use for your inspections.

When you make quality assurance audits a part of your regular routine, you will be benefiting yourself, your company, and your employees.

There are many options and choices, so you can make it simple to perform quality inspections. These audits will help you to provide excellent customer service and quality so you can build a strong reputation and grow your business.

Conclusion

My biggest fear when starting a cleaning business ten years ago was not having real job security. However, I soon realized I could develop my own job security by calling the shots and making my own business decisions. Starting a cleaning business helped me to achieve security.

After ten years, I've gone from a simple residential cleaning business where I did all the work to a full schedule with large contracts that include both residential and commercial buildings. This is because I have steady work, great pay, and plenty of free time to pursue my personal goals.

I admit that I was initially drawn to the idea of working for myself, but wasn't entirely sure what I was getting into. In addition to my concern about job security, I also doubted my cleaning skills. When I started with just a few small residential jobs, it was a great way to strengthen my skills and get me more comfortable with my job.

That's when I realized I really didn't mind cleaning if I was getting paid well for it. I enjoyed the satisfaction of leaving behind a neat and clean home. Perhaps best of all, I enjoyed being my own boss.

Then I expanded and started to research cleaning tips and business ideas. I learned how to do other types of cleaning, so I could expand my business into other areas. This has improved my job security.

Now that I have employees and a strong business, I can look back on those early days as the best decision of my life.

11 Core Benefits of Owning Your Business

If you are still on the fence about starting a cleaning business, then let me finish by telling you of the eleven benefits I now enjoy from running my own cleaning business.

Potential for Unlimited Income

There is no limit to how far you grow your cleaning business. I built mine from a one-person residential cleaning company into an over $250,000 a year business with 22 employees. And I still have the potential to grow more. You can't do this with many jobs. Cleaning isn't a complicated or expensive business to start.

Quick Revenue

After the initial planning and legal phases are complete, you can often get your first clients within days. Within weeks you'll be quoting and bidding on jobs. By the second week, you'll be doing your first job and bringing in revenue. Then you'll have a full business within a month.

Start on a Budget

You often don't need over $500 to start a cleaning business. This makes it an excellent inexpensive start-up. I started with just a vacuum, car, and some cleaning supplies.

Be Your Own Boss

This is my personal favorite benefit for starting a cleaning business. When I'm my own boss, I can be sure I'm going in the right direction with my life. There will be mistakes, but you can learn from them and make your business stronger.

Determine Your Own Hours

This is another great aspect of starting your own business. You can take days off when you want as long as you can still make a decent income. You can work smarter instead of harder so you can free up time on your schedule.

Daily Paychecks

This is the second-best thing I enjoy aside from being my own boss. I get a check at least once a day, if not more. This means I don't have to stress about my jobs being paid on time. I don't have to wait every two weeks or once a month to get my paycheck. This means less stress and more time to enjoy life.

Easy Work that Isn't Technical or Complicated

Starting a house cleaning business doesn't tax your brain. Whether you prefer to use your brain or not, a house cleaning business is a perfect fit. In fact, some people enjoy the gentle, repetitive tasks involved in cleaning.

No Mental or Emotional Exhaustion

Think about your current job and how emotionally draining it can be. This makes it hard to follow creative endeavors and makes life very frustrating. You are tired a lot of the time, and motivation can be difficult. Once you start your own business, you can focus on your lifelong desires in your free time since you will be running a part-time cleaning business.

Choosing Who You Work With

This is another wonderful benefit. Again think about your current job. There are individuals you enjoy being around, and they make work enjoyable. On the other hand, there is always that one co-worker who makes work a drag. When you own your own business, you can choose who you hire, and if someone doesn't work out, then you will be able to do something about it.

Work from Home

This may not be entirely the case. If you prefer, you can work from home, especially if you have space for it. As you grow your business, you may find that have a retail location is best. However, for a while, it is nice to enjoy the benefits of working from home and not having to put up with the daily commute.

Start Additional Cleaning Services

You can maximize your profits by adding on any number of additional cleaning services. This can include carpet cleaning, steam cleaning, or any other number of specialized services I discussed earlier. You can even branch out into pet sitting and house sitting if you want.

Starting a cleaning business may not seem that glamorous, but it can be profitable and enjoyable.

You gain more free time, have a less stressful life, and this all makes you more productive. So hopefully, after all this, I've convinced you to at least give it a try part-time while deciding if quitting your full-time job to start your own cleaning business is the best option for you.

If you need to get in touch with me for any reason, feel free to email me at csbapublishing@gmail.com

SAMPLE CLEANING SERVICES AGREEMENT

(NOTE: If you need to download any of these forms, please email us at csbapublishing@gmail.com.)

THIS CLEANING SERVICES AGREEMENT (the "Agreement") dated this _____ day of _____, _____

BETWEEN:

James Doe Corp. of 999 A Street, Any town, Colorado, 12345
(the "Client")

- AND -

Carmen Cleaning Services of 123 Main Street, Any town, Colorado, 12345
(the "Contractor").

BACKGROUND:

A. The Client is of the opinion that the Contractor has the necessary qualifications, experience, and abilities to provide services to the Client.
B. The Contractor is agreeable to providing such services to the Client on the terms and conditions set out in this Agreement.

IN CONSIDERATION OF the matters described above and of the mutual benefits and obligations set forth in this Agreement, the receipt and sufficiency of which consideration is hereby acknowledged, the Client and the Contractor (individually the "Party" and collectively the "Parties" to this Agreement) agree as follows:

Services Provided

1. The Client hereby agrees to engage the Contractor to provide the Client with services (the "Services") consisting of:
    - clean and sanitize restroom facilities; sweep, mop, and wax floors; vacuum and shampoo carpets; empty, clean, and sanitize waste receptacles.
2. The Services will also include any other tasks which the Parties may agree on. The Contractor hereby agrees to provide such Services to the Client.

Term of Agreement

3. The term of this Agreement (the "Term") will begin on the date of this Agreement and will remain in full force and effect indefinitely until terminated as provided in this Agreement.
4. In the event that either Party wishes to terminate this Agreement, that Party will be required to provide 90 days' written notice to the other Party.
5. This Agreement may be terminated at any time by mutual agreement of the Parties.
6. Except as otherwise provided in this Agreement, the obligations of the Contractor

will end upon the termination of this Agreement.

Performance

7. The Parties agree to do everything necessary to ensure that the terms of this Agreement take effect.

Currency

8. Except as otherwise provided in this Agreement, all monetary amounts referred to in this Agreement are in USD (US Dollars).

Compensation

9. For the services rendered by the Contractor as required by this Agreement, the Client will provide compensation (the "Compensation") to the Contractor of $550.00 per week.
10. The Client will be invoiced every two weeks.
11. Invoices submitted by the Contractor to the Client are due within 30 days of receipt.

Reimbursement of Expenses

12. The Contractor will be reimbursed from time to time for reasonable and necessary expenses incurred by the Contractor in connection with providing the Services under this Agreement.
13. All expenses must be pre-approved by the Client.

Penalties for Late Payment

14. Any late payments will trigger a fee of 10.00% per month on the amount still owing.

Confidentiality

15. Confidential information (the "Confidential Information") refers to any data or information relating to the Client, whether business or personal, which would reasonably be considered to be private or proprietary to the Client and that is not generally known and where the release of that Confidential Information could reasonably be expected to cause harm to the Client.
16. The Contractor agrees that they will not disclose, divulge, reveal, report or use, for any purpose, any Confidential Information which the Contractor has obtained, except as authorized by the Client or as required by law. The Cleaning Services Provider further agrees that they will not disclose, divulge, reveal, report or use, for any purpose, any personal information of the Client, without the prior written consent of the Client. The obligations of confidentiality will apply during the term of this Agreement and will survive indefinitely upon termination of this Agreement.

Return of Property

17. Upon the expiry or termination of this Agreement, the Contractor will return to the Client any property, documentation, records,

or Confidential Information, which is the property of the Client.

Capacity/Independent Contractor

18. In providing the Services under this Agreement, it is expressly agreed that the Contractor is acting as an independent contractor and not as an employee. The Contractor and the Client acknowledge that this Agreement does not create a partnership or joint venture between them, and is exclusively a contract for service. The Client is not required to pay or make any contributions to any social security, local, state or federal tax, unemployment compensation, workers' compensation, insurance premium, profit-sharing, pension, or any other employee benefit for the Contractor during the Term. The Contractor is responsible for paying and complying with reporting requirements for all local, state, and federal taxes related to payments made to the Contractor under this Agreement.

Notice

19. All notices, requests, demands, or other communications required or permitted by the terms of this Agreement will be given in writing and delivered to the Parties of this Agreement as follows:
    a. James Doe Corp.
       999 A Street, Any town, Colorado, 12345

    b. Carmen Cleaning Services
       123 Main Street, Any town, Colorado, 12345

or to such other address as any Party may from time to time notify the other, and will be deemed to be properly delivered (a) immediately upon being served personally, (b) two days after being deposited with the postal service if served by registered mail, or (c) the following day after being deposited with an overnight courier.

Indemnification

20. Except to the extent paid in settlement from any applicable insurance policies, and to the extent permitted by applicable law, each Party agrees to indemnify and hold harmless the other Party, and its respective directors, stockholders, affiliates, officers, agents, employees, and permitted successors and assigns against any and all claims, losses, damages, liabilities, penalties, punitive damages, expenses, reasonable legal fees and costs of any kind or amount whatsoever, which result from or arise out of any act or omission of the indemnifying party, its respective directors, stockholders, affiliates, officers, agents, employees, and permitted successors and assigns that occurs in connection with this Agreement. This indemnification will survive the termination of this Agreement.

Modification of Agreement

21. Any amendment or modification of this Agreement or additional obligation assumed by either Party in connection with this Agreement will only be binding if evidenced in writing signed by each Party or an authorized representative of each Party.

Time of the Essence

22. Time is of the essence in this Agreement. No extension or variation of this Agreement will operate as a waiver of this provision.

Assignment

23. The Contractor will not voluntarily, or by operation of law, assign or otherwise transfer its obligations under this Agreement without the prior written consent of the Client.

Entire Agreement

24. It is agreed that there is no representation, warranty, collateral agreement, or condition affecting this Agreement except as expressly provided in this Agreement.

Enurement

25. This Agreement will enure to the benefit of and be binding on the Parties and their respective heirs, executors, administrators and permitted successors and assigns.

Titles/Headings

26. Headings are inserted for the convenience of the Parties only and are not to be considered when interpreting this Agreement.

Gender

27. Words in the singular mean and include the plural and vice versa. Words in the masculine mean and include the feminine and vice versa.

Governing Law

28. It is the intention of the Parties to this Agreement that this Agreement and the performance under this Agreement, and all suits and special proceedings under this Agreement, be construed in accordance with and governed, to the exclusion of the law of any other forum, by the laws of the State of Colorado, without regard to the jurisdiction in which any action or special proceeding may be instituted.

Severability

29. In the event that any of the provisions of this Agreement are held to be invalid or unenforceable in whole or in part, all other provisions will nevertheless continue to be valid and enforceable with the invalid or unenforceable parts severed from the remainder of this Agreement.

Waiver

30. The waiver by either Party of a breach, default, delay, or omission of any of the provisions of this Agreement by the other Party will not be construed as a waiver of any subsequent breach of the same or other provisions.

IN WITNESS WHEREOF the Parties have duly affixed their signatures under hand and seal on this _____ day of _____, _____.

Sample LLC/S Operating Agreement

OPERATING AGREEMENT
of
Green Cleaning Services

This Operating Agreement (the "Agreement") made and entered into this _____ day of _____, _____ (the "Execution Date"),

BY:

Maria Carmen of 123 Main Street, Any Town, Colorado 12345

(the "Member").

BACKGROUND:

A. The Member wishes to be the sole member of a limited liability company.
B. The terms and conditions of this Agreement will govern the Member within the limited liability company.

IN CONSIDERATION OF and as a condition of the Member entering into this Agreement and other valuable consideration, the receipt and sufficiency of which is acknowledged, the Member agrees as follows:

Formation

1. By this Agreement, the Member forms a Limited Liability Company (the "Company")

in accordance with the laws of the State of Colorado. The rights and obligations of the Member will be as stated in the Colorado Limited Liability Company Act (the "Act") except as otherwise provided in this agreement.

Name

2. The name of the Company will be Green Cleaning Services.

Sole Member

3. While the Company consists only of one Member, any reference in this Agreement to two or more Members and that requires the majority consent or unanimous consent of Members, or that requires a certain percentage vote of Members, should be interpreted as only requiring the consent or vote of the sole Member.

Purpose

4. Janitorial and Cleaning.

Term

5. The Company will continue until terminated as provided in this Agreement or may dissolve under conditions provided in the Act.

Place of Business

6. The Principal Office of the Company will be located at 123 Main Street, Any Town,

Colorado 12345, or such other place as the Members may from time to time designate.

Capital Contributions

7. The following table shows the Initial Contributions of the Member. The Member agrees to make the Initial Contributions to the Company in full, according to the following terms:

Member	Contribution Description	Value of Contribution
Maria Carmen	TBD	$5,000.00

Allocation of Profits/Losses

8. Subject to the other provisions of this Agreement, the Net Profits or Losses, for both accounting and tax purposes, will accrue to and be borne by the sole Member:

   Maria Carmen of 123 Main Street, Any Town, Colorado 12345.
9. No Member will have priority over any other Member for the distribution of Net Profits or Losses.

Nature of Interest

10. A Member's Interest in the Company will be considered personal property.

Withdrawal of Contribution

11. No Member will withdraw any portion of their Capital Contribution without the unanimous consent of the other Members.

Liability for Contribution

12. A Member's obligation to make their required Capital Contribution can only be compromised or released with the consent of all remaining Members or as otherwise provided in this Agreement. If a Member does not make the Capital Contribution when it is due, he is obligated at the option of any remaining Members to contribute cash equal to the agreed value of the Capital Contribution. This option is in addition to and not in lieu of any other rights, including the right to specific performance that the Company may have against the Member.

Additional Contributions

13. Capital Contributions may be amended from time to time, according to the business needs of the Company. However, if additional capital is determined to be required and an individual Member is unwilling or unable to meet the additional contribution requirement within a reasonable period, the remaining Members may contribute in proportion to their existing Capital Contributions to resolve the amount in default. In such case, the allocation of Net Profits or Losses and the distribution of

assets on dissociation or dissolution will be adjusted accordingly.

14. Any advance of money to the Company by any Member in excess of the amounts provided for in this Agreement or subsequently agreed to, will be deemed a debt due from the Company rather than an increase in the Capital Contribution of the Member. This liability will be repaid with interest at such rates and times to be determined by a majority of the Members. This liability will not entitle the lending Member to any increased share of the Company's profits nor to greater voting power. Repayment of such debts will have priority over any other payments to Members.

Capital Accounts

15. An individual capital account (the "Capital Account") will be maintained for each Member, and their Initial Contributions will be credited to this account. Any Additional Contributions made by any Member will be credited to that Member's individual Capital Account.

Interest on Capital

16. No borrowing charge or loan interest will be due or payable to any Member on their agreed Capital Contribution inclusive of any agreed Additional Contributions.

Management

17. Management of this Company is vested in the Members.

Authority to Bind Company

18. Only the following individuals have the authority to bind the Company in contract: The Manager.

Duty of Loyalty

19. While a person is a Member of the Company, and for a period of at least five years after that person ceases to be a Member, that person will not carry on, or participate in, a similar business to the business of the Company within any market regions that were established or contemplated by the Company before or during that person's tenure as Member.

Duty to Devote Time

20. Each Member will devote such time and attention to the business of the Company as the majority of the Members will, from time to time, reasonably determine for the conduct of the Company's business.

Member Meetings

21. A meeting may be called by any Member providing that reasonable notice has been given to the other Members.
22. Regular meetings of the Members will be held only as required.

Voting

23. Each Member will be entitled to cast votes on any matter based upon the proportion of that Member's Capital Contributions in the Company.

Admission of New Members

24. A new Member may only be admitted to the Company with a majority vote of the existing Members.
25. The new Member agrees to be bound by all the covenants, terms, and conditions of this Agreement, inclusive of all current and future amendments. Further, a new Member will execute such documents as are needed to effect the admission of the new Member. Any new Member will receive such business interest in the Company as determined by a unanimous decision of the other Members.

Voluntary Withdrawal of a Member

26. No Member may voluntarily withdraw from the Company for a period of one year from the execution date of this Agreement. Any such unauthorized withdrawal prior to the expiration of this period will be considered a wrongful dissociation and a breach of this Agreement. In the event of any such wrongful dissociation, the withdrawing Member will be liable to the remaining Members for any damages incurred by the remaining Members including but not limited to the loss of future earnings. After the expiration of this period, any Member will have the right to withdraw from the

Company voluntarily. Written notice of intention to withdraw must be served upon the remaining Members at least three months prior to withdrawal.
27. The voluntary withdrawal of a Member will have no effect upon the continuance of the Company.
28. It remains incumbent on the withdrawing Member to exercise this dissociation in good faith and to minimize any present or future harm done to the remaining Members as a result of the withdrawal.

Involuntary Withdrawal of a Member

29. Events leading to the involuntary withdrawal of a Member from the Company will include but not be limited to: death of a Member; Member mental incapacity; Member disability preventing reasonable participation in the Company; Member incompetence; breach of fiduciary duties by a Member; criminal conviction of a Member; Operation of Law against a Member or a legal judgment against a Member that can reasonably be expected to bring the business or societal reputation of the Company into disrepute. Expulsion of a Member can also occur on application by the Company or another Member, where it has been judicially determined that the Member: has engaged in wrongful conduct that adversely and materially affected the Company's business; has willfully or persistently committed a material breach of this Agreement or of a duty owed to the Company or to the other

Members; or has engaged in conduct relating to the Company's business that makes it not reasonably practicable to carry on the business with the Member.
30. The involuntary withdrawal of a Member will have no effect upon the continuance of the Company.

Dissociation of a Member

31. Where the Company consists of two or more Members, in the event of either a voluntary or involuntary withdrawal of a Member, if the remaining Members elect to purchase the interest of the withdrawing Member, the remaining Members will serve written notice of such election, including the purchase price and method and schedule of payment for the withdrawing Member's Interests, upon the withdrawing Member, their executor, administrator, trustee, committee or analogous fiduciary within a reasonable period after acquiring knowledge of the change in circumstance to the affected Member. The purchase amount of any buyout of a Member's Interests will be determined as set out in the Valuation of Interest section of this Agreement.
32. Valuation and distribution will be determined as described in the Valuation of Interest section of this Agreement.
33. The remaining Members retain the right to seek damages from a dissociated Member where the dissociation resulted from a malicious or criminal act by the dissociated Member or where the dissociated Member

had breached their fiduciary duty to the Company or was in breach of this Agreement or had acted in a way that could reasonably be foreseen to bring harm or damage to the Company or to the reputation of the Company.

34. A dissociated Member will only have liability for Company obligations that were incurred during their time as a Member. On dissociation of a Member, the Company will prepare, file, serve, and publish all notices required by law to protect the dissociated Member from liability for future Company obligations.

35. Where the remaining Members have purchased the interest of a dissociated Member, the purchase amount will be paid in full, but without interest, within 90 days of the date of withdrawal. The Company will retain exclusive rights to use of the trade name and firm name and all related brand and model names of the Company.

Right of First Purchase

36. Where the Company consists of two or more Members, in the event that a Member's Interest in the Company is or will be sold, due to any reason, the remaining Members will have a right of first purchase of that Member's Interest. The value of that interest in the Company will be the lower of the value set out in the Valuation of Interest section of this Agreement and any third party offer that the Member wishes to accept.

Assignment of Interest

37. A Member's financial interest in the Company can only be assigned to another Member and cannot be assigned to a third party except with the unanimous consent of the remaining Members.
38. In the event that a Member's interest in the company is transferred or assigned as the result of a court order or Operation of Law, the trustee in bankruptcy or other person acquiring that Member's Interests in the Company will only acquire that Member's economic rights and interests and will not acquire any other rights of that Member or be admitted as a Member of the Company or have the right to exercise any management or voting interests.

Valuation of Interest

39. A Member's financial interest in the Company will be in proportion to their Capital Contributions, inclusive of any Additional Capital Contributions.
40. In the absence of a written agreement setting a value, the value of the Company will be based on the fair market value appraisal of all Company assets (less liabilities) determined in accordance with generally accepted accounting principles (GAAP). This appraisal will be conducted by an independent accounting firm agreed to by all Members. An appraiser will be appointed within a reasonable period of the date of withdrawal or dissolution. The results of the

appraisal will be binding on all Members. The intent of this section is to ensure the survival of the Company despite the withdrawal of any individual Member.
41. No allowance will be made for goodwill, trade name, patents, or other intangible assets, except where those assets have been reflected on the Company books immediately prior to valuation.

Dissolution

42. The Company may be dissolved by a unanimous vote of the Members. The Company will also be dissolved on the occurrence of events specified in the Act.
43. Upon Dissolution of the Company and liquidation of Company property, and after payment of all selling costs and expenses, the liquidator will distribute the Company assets to the following groups according to the following order of priority:
    a. in satisfaction of liabilities to creditors except Company obligations to current Members;
    b. in satisfaction of Company debt obligations to current Members; and then
    c. to the Members based on Member financial interest, as set out in the Valuation of Interest section of this Agreement.

Records

44. The Company will at all times maintain accurate records of the following:
    a. Information regarding the status of the business and the financial condition of the Company.
    b. A copy of the Company's federal, state, and local income taxes for each year, promptly after becoming available.
    c. Name and last known business, residential, or mailing address of each Member, as well as the date that person became a Member.
    d. A copy of this Agreement and any articles or certificate of formation, as well as all amendments, together with any executed copies of any written powers of attorney pursuant to which this Agreement, articles or certificate, and any amendments have been executed.
    e. The cash, property, and services contributed to the Company by each Member, along with with a description and value, and any contributions that have been agreed to be made in the future.
45. Each Member has the right to demand, within a reasonable period of time, a copy of any of the above documents for any purpose reasonably related to their interest as a Member of the Company, at their expense.

Books of Account

46. Accurate and complete books of account of the transactions of the Company will be kept in accordance with generally accepted accounting principles (GAAP) and at all reasonable times will be available and open to inspection and examination by any Member. The books and records of the Company will reflect all the Company's transactions and will be appropriate and adequate for the business conducted by the Company.

Banking and Company Funds

47. The funds of the Company will be placed in such investments and banking accounts as will be designated by the Members. All withdrawals from these accounts will be made by the duly authorized agent or agents of the Company as appointed by the unanimous consent of the Members. Company funds will be held in the name of the Company and will not be commingled with those of any other person or entity.

Audit

48. Any of the Members will have the right to request an audit of the Company books. The cost of the audit will be borne by the Company. The audit will be performed by an accounting firm acceptable to all the Members. Not more than one (1) audit will be required by any or all of the Members for any fiscal year.

Tax Treatment

49. This Company is intended to be treated as a disregarded entity for the purposes of Federal and State Income Tax.

Annual Report

50. As soon as practicable after the close of each fiscal year, the Company will furnish to each Member an annual report showing a full and complete account of the condition of the Company, including all information as will be necessary for the preparation of each Member's income or other tax returns. This report will consist of at least:
    a. A copy of the Company's federal income tax returns for that fiscal year.
    b. Income statement.

Goodwill

51. The goodwill of the Company will be assessed at an amount to be determined by appraisal using generally accepted accounting principles (GAAP).

Governing Law

52. The Members submit to the jurisdiction of the courts of the State of Colorado for the enforcement of this Agreement or any arbitration award or decision arising from this Agreement.

Force Majeure

53. A Member will be free of liability to the Company where the Member is prevented from executing their obligations under this

Agreement in whole or in part due to force majeure, such as earthquake, typhoon, flood, fire, and war or any other unforeseen and uncontrollable event where the Member has communicated the circumstance of the event to any and all other Members and where the Member has taken any and all appropriate action to satisfy his duties and obligations to the Company and to mitigate the effects of the event.

Forbidden Acts

54. No Member may do any act in contravention of this Agreement.
55. No Member may permit, intentionally or unintentionally, the assignment of express, implied, or apparent authority to a third party that is not a Member of the Company.
56. No Member may do any act that would make it impossible to carry on the ordinary business of the Company.
57. No Member will have the right or authority to bind or obligate the Company to any extent with regard to any matter outside the intended purpose of the Company.
58. No Member may confess a judgment against the Company.
59. Any violation of the above-forbidden acts will be deemed an Involuntary Withdrawal and may be treated accordingly by the remaining Members.

Indemnification

60. All Members will be indemnified and held harmless by the Company from and against any and all claims of any nature, whatsoever, arising out of a Member's participation in Company affairs. A Member will not be entitled to indemnification under this section for liability arising out of gross negligence or willful misconduct of the Member or the breach by the Member of any provisions of this Agreement.

Liability

61. A Member or any employee will not be liable to the Company or to any other Member for any mistake or error in judgment or for any act or omission believed in good faith to be within the scope of authority conferred or implied by this Agreement or the Company. The Member or employee will be liable only for any and all acts and omissions involving intentional wrongdoing.

Liability Insurance

62. The Company may acquire insurance on behalf of any Member, employee, agent, or other person engaged in the business interest of the Company against any liability asserted against them or incurred by them while acting in good faith on behalf of the Company.

Life Insurance

63. The Company will have the right to acquire life insurance on the lives of any or all of the

Members, whenever it is deemed necessary by the Company. Each Member will cooperate fully with the Company in obtaining any such policies of life insurance.

Actions Requiring Unanimous Consent

64. The following actions will require the unanimous consent of all Members:
    a. Endangering the ownership or possession of Company property, including selling, transferring, or loaning any Company property or using any Company property as collateral for a loan.

Amendment of this Agreement

65. No amendment or modification of this Agreement will be valid or effective unless in writing and signed by all Members.

Title to Company Property

66. Title to all Company property will remain in the name of the Company. No Member or group of Members will have any ownership interest in Company property in whole or in part.

Miscellaneous

67. Time is of the essence in this Agreement.
68. This Agreement may be executed in counterparts.
69. Headings are inserted for the convenience of the Members only and are not to be considered when interpreting this

Agreement. Words in the singular mean and include the plural and vice versa. Words in the masculine gender include the feminine gender and vice versa. Words in a neutral gender include the masculine gender and the feminine gender and vice versa.

70. If any term, covenant, condition or provision of this Agreement is held by a court of competent jurisdiction to be invalid, void or unenforceable, it is the Members' intent that such provision be reduced in scope by the court only to the extent deemed necessary by that court to render the provision reasonable and enforceable, and the remainder of the provisions of this Agreement will in no way be affected, impaired or invalidated as a result.

71. This Agreement contains the entire agreement between the Members. All negotiations and understandings have been included in this Agreement. Statements or representations that may have been made by any Member during the negotiation stages of this Agreement may, in some way, be inconsistent with this final written Agreement. All such statements have no force or effect with respect to this Agreement. Only the written terms of this Agreement will bind the Members.

72. This Agreement and the terms and conditions contained in this Agreement apply to and are binding upon each Member's successors, assigns, executors, administrators, beneficiaries, and representatives.

73. Any notices or delivery required here will be deemed completed when hand-delivered, delivered by agent, or seven (7) days after being placed in the post, postage prepaid, to the Members at the addresses contained in this Agreement or as the Members may later designate in writing.
74. All of the rights, remedies, and benefits provided by this Agreement will be cumulative and will not be exclusive of any other such rights, remedies, and benefits allowed by law.

Definitions

75. For the purpose of this Agreement, the following terms are defined as follows:
    a. "Additional Contribution" means Capital Contributions, other than Initial Contributions, made by Members to the Company.
    b. "Capital Contribution" means the total amount of cash, property, or services contributed to the Company by any one Member.
    c. "Distributions" means a payment of Company profits to the Members.
    d. "Initial Contribution" means the initial Capital Contributions made by any Member to acquire an interest in the Company.
    e. "Member's Interests" means the Member's collective rights, including but not limited to, the Member's right to share in profits, Member's right to a share of Company assets on the

dissolution of the Company, Member's voting rights, and Member's rights to participate in the management of the Company.
f. "Net Profits or Losses" means the net profits or losses of the Company as determined by generally accepted accounting principles (GAAP).
g. "Operation of Law" means rights or duties that are cast upon a party by the law, without any act or agreement on the part of the individual, including, but not limited to, an assignment for the benefit of creditors, a divorce, or a bankruptcy.
h. "Principal Office" means the office, whether inside or outside the State of Colorado, where the executive or management of the Company maintains their primary office.
i. "Voting Members" means the Members who belong to a membership class that has voting power. Where there is only one class of Members, then those Members constitute the Voting Members.

IN WITNESS WHEREOF the Member has duly affixed their signature under hand and seal on this _____ day of _____, _____.

Sample Business Plan

1.0 Executive Summary

Introduction

Green Cleaning Services is a new cleaning service specializing in office cleaning and serving the Denver, Colorado area. The business will sell office cleaning and related services to businesses with office spaces of any size. To that end, Green Cleaning Services seeks funding for equipment and initial operations of the business.

The Company

Established in 2006, the business offers office cleaning, floor treatment, carpet cleaning, and window cleaning for businesses with office space in the Denver area. The business was founded by Maria Carmen and Jane Doe, who have pooled their resources to develop a new strategy for reaching and serving business clients. The business will operate out of a central office and storage facility and use the labor of trained cleaning crews to serve clients.

Services

Services offered will be based around basic office cleaning scheduled on a monthly basis, which will be offered with extreme care for the client's privacy, security, and assets. Additional services will be sold to the same clients to deepen their relationship with Green Cleaning services will be introduced in after three years. Services will be environmentally friendly, both in the products used and in their methods of disposal.

The Market

The market currently consists of 47,000 small, medium, and large office businesses. Healthy growth is expected for this market, especially for small offices, which will be the initial target market for the business. Focusing on small offices will establish the reputation of the company by working with a variety of clients and will force the streamlining of operations.

Financial Results

The business expects to reach $1 million in annual sales in its second year of operation. A net profit of $70,000 will be achieved in the first year and will double in the second year. Break-even will be achieved quickly partially due to the fact that the management is experienced with sales, marketing, and operations, and that all cleaning crews will be paid only for hours worked, reducing the payroll risk for the business.

Chart: Highlights

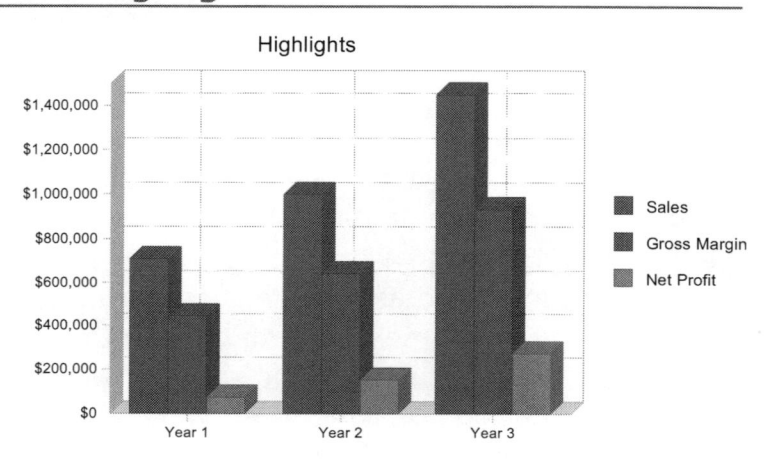

1.1 Objectives

Green Cleaning Services seeks to establish itself as a leader in office cleaning in the Denver, CO area. Specific objectives we will seek to meet over the next two years include:

6. To build a substantial, regular client base of 100 clients on monthly cleaning plans, for a total of over 800,000 square feet of office cleaning each month.
7. To build operations infrastructure, including a central headquarters, 5 delivery vans, professional management, and documented processes for operations and cleaning practices.
8. To build healthy gross margins by establishing itself as a significant buyer and reducing vendor pricing on cleaning supplies and by training low-cost labor to be more productive.
9. To create a culture of productivity and resourcefulness for all staff by encouraging the best ideas and cleaning procedures to rise to the top and rewarding cleaning crew for their contributions.

1.2 Mission

Green Cleaning Services seeks to ensure that businesses have a spotless office environment to support the work they do and forget their worries about office cleaning. The company values its employees for cleaning well and cleaning smart, listening to the needs of its clients, and responding to the demands of the environment.

1.3 Keys to Success

To become successful in the office cleaning business, Green Cleaning Services must:

- Foster an environment of employee empowerment from day one of operation to make sure cleaning crews clean well (thoroughly and carefully) while cleaning smart (efficiently)
- Listen attentively to the needs of the client and communicate this information effectively to cleaning crews
- Research and remain experts on the greenest cleaning practices and products
- Remember that the cleaning must meet or exceed client expectations to be considered done

2.0 Company Summary

Green Cleaning Services is an office cleaning business located in Denver, MO. Established in 2009, the business offers office cleaning, floor treatment, carpet cleaning, and window cleaning for businesses with office space in the Denver area. The business was founded by Maria Carmen and Jane Doe, two cleaning industry professionals with decades of collective experience, who have pooled their resources to develop a new strategy for reaching and serving business clients.

2.1 Company Ownership

Green Cleaning Services is an S Corporation currently owned 51% by Maria Carmen and 49% by Jane Doe, the founders, and directors of the company. Once the additional investment has been contributed by angel investors, those investors will own 49% of the business, Maria Carmen will own 26%, and Jane Doe will own 25%.

2.2 Start-up Summary

The startup expenses for the business reflect the legal permitting required in the state of Colorado, the legal agreements with additional investors and banks for financing, two month's security deposit at an estimated $2,500 per month and one month's rent for improvements to the office and storage facility, improvements including lighting fixtures, storage cabinets, and sinks, and office supplies and computer supplies for three workstations (two founders and one administrator).

Assets that must be purchased include office furniture and computers for the office, cleaning equipment including buffing machines, vacuums, and basic tools (mops, brooms, buckets, etc.) and one delivery van.

Some of the larger pieces of equipment can be purchased with seller-financing, such as the delivery van and buffing machines. Otherwise, it is most economical or required to pay for these expenses and assets in cash.

Table: Start-up

Legal	$2,000
Stationery	$2,000
Insurance	$3,000

Rent	$7,500
Computer Systems	$5,000
Office Supplies	$2,000
Facility Leasehold Improvements	$10,000
Other	$2,000
Total Start-up Expenses	$33,500
Start-up Assets	
Cash Required	$60,000
Other Current Assets	$5,000
Long-term Assets	$40,000
Total Assets	$105,000
Total Requirements	$138,500

Chart: Start-up

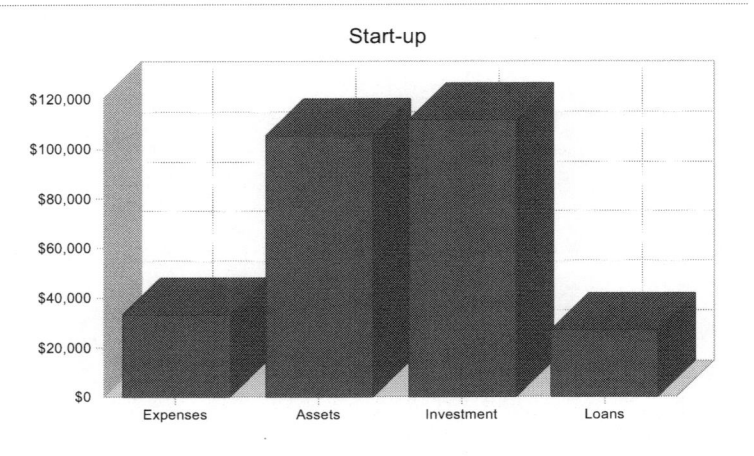

3.0 Services

Services to be offered by Green Cleaning Services will focus specifically on office spaces and include:

1. Office cleaning (including garbage removal, dusting, and cleaning of all surfaces, sweeping and mopping of floors, and cleaning of doors and walls as needed)
2. Furniture cleaning
3. Floor waxing
4. Floor stripping and sealing
5. Carpet cleaning
6. Window cleaning
7. Bathroom and kitchen area cleaning

In the future, Green Cleaning Services will provide office organization and decluttering services through an interior designer. This service will be provided as an upsell to this foundation of services.

4.0 Market Analysis Summary

The market for office cleaning in the Denver area includes small offices (1-5 employees), medium offices (6-20 employees), and large offices (21 employees and up). In the Denver area, businesses with offices are growing as the service sector increases, with a net of 3,000 new businesses established in 2008. Due to the economic renewal occurring in this community, this growth is expected to continue over the next two years. Small offices are targeted as well as large, although margins will be lower due to the increased amount spent on sales and travel relative to medium and large offices, because many small businesses will expand, giving Green Cleaning Services a foothold in this market by the time competitors are willing to sell to them.

4.1 Market Segmentation

The market for Green Cleaning Services is comprised of small offices, medium offices, and large offices in the Denver area.

Small Offices: Either newly established ventures or small businesses designed to remain small, few cleaning businesses seek to serve this market because of the cost in doing so. Therefore, business owners generally require employees to do their own cleaning, assuming they are saving money through this work. Green Cleaning Services must show these businesses not only that they do not save money by having employees do this work, but that by having professional cleaners maintain their offices they will increase morale, productivity, and their appearance to customers if customers/clients enter their office spaces.

Medium Offices: This group has a growing acceptance of the need for professional cleaning services and is concerned primarily about the price.

Large Offices: This group accepts the need to outsource their office cleaning to professionals and is interested in working with vendors who can handle specific requests and take care to protect the information, security, and equipment within their office spaces.

Chart: Market Analysis (Pie)

Market Analysis (Pie)

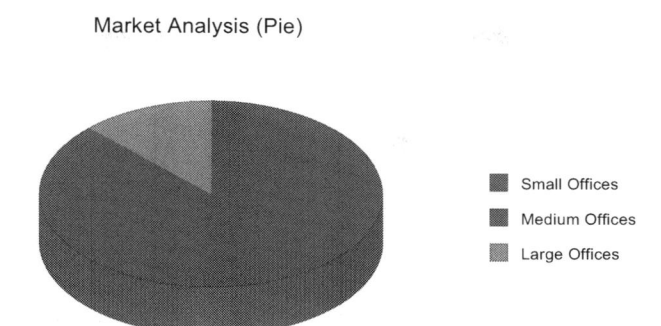

- Small Offices
- Medium Offices
- Large Offices

4.2 Target Market Segment Strategy

Green Cleaning Services will build its expertise from the ground up, by building a successful base of small-office clients, moving on to medium-office clients and then large-office clients. While larger clients will not be turned away as the business starts out, it is expected that they will be more likely to use Green Cleaning Services after its record of customer service and operational success is established by work with numerous smaller clients. Furthermore, by working with smaller clients first, the business will establish a foothold faster as they will not be competing directly with established cleaning companies at first, and will be able to work towards making this group more profitable through economies of scale and tight operations.

Green Cleaning Services will not work for landlords, providing building janitorial services. Many firms specialize in this service already, and marketing janitorial services to buildings involves different promotional activities, operations, and cleaning skills, to a certain extent. By specializing in commercial office cleaning, Green Cleaning Services will increase its ability to market to the many thousands of area businesses directly.

4.3 Service Business Analysis

The office cleaning industry includes many local companies, as well as some national franchises. Services are purchased directly by business managers and owners for small businesses and by purchasing agents, office managers, and procurement specialists for larger businesses. Businesses desire ongoing relationships with cleaning vendors where they do not have to worry about the cleaning process, but will be concerned if they are paying higher than market rates. Businesses appreciate the ability of a company to quote monthly cleaning rates to make costs less variable, but also to handle special cleaning requests as they arise. Cleaning vendors are sought out through internet searches, the yellow pages, and business referrals.

Financial analysts report that the commercial cleaning industry is recession-resistant and highly stable. Commercial cleaning overall was an $80 billion industry in 2008 and is one of the fastest-growing industries in the US, with projected growth to $150 billion per year by 2010.

4.3.1 Competition and Buying Patterns

The commercial cleaning industry is very fragmented, with no one company owning more than 6% of the market. Franchises account for 10% of the market, and local companies account for 90%. Top franchises include JAN-PRO Cleaning Systems, ServiceMaster Clean, MTOclean, the Cleaning Authority, and MARBLELIFE. Economies of scale for franchises are obtained through unified operations systems, national marketing campaigns, and somewhat through volume discounts from suppliers.

Customers seek out cleaning services based on a combination of reputation, price, and depth of services offered. While large offices value depth of services more so, smaller firms put a greater value on price.

5.0 Strategy and Implementation Summary

Green Cleaning Services has selected the following priorities for its rollout strategy:

- To begin by targeting small offices to gain a foothold in the Denver office cleaning market.
- To leverage the reputation and experience from work with small offices to increasingly seek medium and large office clients in the third year of operation.
- To rapidly scale up organizational infrastructure, including cleaning crews, equipment, and vans.

5.1 Competitive Edge

Green Cleaning Services will develop a competitive edge based on its utilization of the skills, ideas, and productivity of its employees. By encouraging and rewarding employee initiative and ingenuity to discover the best ways to clean well and smart, morale will be increased, making Green Cleaning Services a more desirable place to work. The reputation of the firm as a great place to work will increase application rates and the strength of new hires, reducing the costs of turnover and training. Customer satisfaction will increase, and costs will drop due to this focus on employee utilization.

Initial training by Maria Carmen and Jane Doe will be for cleaning crew heads. This will be ten hours of training in Green Cleaning Services methods for experienced cleaning personnel. Cleaning crew heads will each provide ten hours of training, in turn, for new members of their cleaning crews when they are brought in to the business, based both on Green Cleaning Services methods and basic cleaning skills (depending on the current skills of the crew member).

All client information about the cleaning will be transferred to a detailed job sheet, which will be discussed with the cleaning crew head before reaching the job site. The cleaning crew head will go through a tour and inspection of the job site while the client is present to ensure that the job sheet is complete and that all information about keys, security, and access is understood. Cleanings will always be run by a cleaning crew head and a crew of one to four members. After the crew have experience on a site, a cleaning crew head may move between a few job sites to supervise a greater number of jobs over one day.

5.2 Marketing Strategy

The marketing strategy for Green Cleaning Services begins with its initial target market of small offices.

Promotional activities in the startup phase will include:

    1. Local Trade Show Booths at Office Services and Entrepreneurial trade shows
    2. Blogging, Newsletters, and Microblogging to establish Green Cleaning Services as thought leaders in office cleaning
    3. Prospecting by phone to cold and warm leads
    4. Business networking to generate qualified leads
    5. Coupons for free trials for new businesses passed on through the local Small Business Development Center and Chamber of Commerce

From the startup period onward, the following promotional activities will be important:

    1. Search engine marketing through text ads around office cleaning keywords in the local area
    2. Search engine optimization to improve organic search rankings
    3. Yellow page listing
    4. Local TV commercials

These ongoing promotional activities are reflected as marketing expenses on the Green Cleaning Services Profit and Loss statement.

5.3 Sales Strategy

Sales will be managed by co-founder Maria Carmen. Maria Carmen expects about ten small business clients from her previous work at Clean-Pro to move to Green Cleaning Services upon learning of their value proposition. This will account for a starting base of clients for the business.

The sales process will begin with a short phone conversation to go over the basics of the services offered and to qualify the customer as one interested in regular cleanings. An in-person meeting at the customer's office will follow, after which a proposal for a monthly rate for cleaning will be given. A follow up with the client will occur after the first three regular cleanings to get additional feedback and to continue to adjust the directions to the cleaning crew.

Before inquiries begin to come in through advertising, Maria will prospect for sales through business networking, cold calls, and warm calls. Green Cleaning Services expects 5% of cold calls, 20% of warm calls, and 30% of networking leads to yield regular customers.

As a partner in the business, Maria will be compensated through a base salary, dividends, and appreciation of the company's stock. After two years of operation, an additional salaried salesperson will be hired who will be compensated for sales through quarterly bonuses, and Maria will remain sales manager.

5.3.1 Sales Forecast

Growth is expected to speed up rapidly over the first two years as small-office customers are sought out and sold to. After the first two years, growth slows as operations must be continually increased to allow for greater growth.

However, the additional target market of medium and large offices will be accessed starting in the third year of operation. Sales will be driven by the basic office cleaning service. Based on the previous success of Maria Carmen as a seller of commercial cleaning, these projections are reasonable, as Maria sold $2 million in cleaning services in his last full year at JAN-PRO. The additional services will be sold as add-ons to clients who purchase office cleaning. It is estimated that 50% of clients will purchase some additional services.

The forecast is also supported by the fact that, after the first year of operations, medium offices will be targeted as well, increasing the rate of growth as each sale will bring higher square footage of space to clean.

Direct costs include the labor of cleaning crew members and the cleaning crew head, cleaning supplies and gasoline, or other transit costs for crew and equipment. Cleaning Crew Head supervision of jobs is expected to cost 5% of sales, and Cleaning Crew (Hourly) wages for the execution of cleanings are expected to cost 27.5% of sales.

To ensure that sales are profitable, Maria will not be compensated on commission by sales, but by profits, after a reasonable base salary. This will keep gross margins around the industry average of 68%.

Table: Sales Forecast

Sales Forecast			
	Year 1	Year 2	Year 3
Unit Sales			
Office Cleaning (1000 Square Feet)	5,014	8,000	12,000
Window Cleaning (10 Windows)	807	1,000	1,250
Floor Treatments	991	1,500	2,000
Carpet Cleaning (100 Square Feet)	1,304	1,000	1,250
Bathroom and Kitchen Cleaning (By Room)	528	500	600
Total Unit Sales	8,643	12,000	17,100

Unit Prices	Year 1	Year 2	Year 3
Office Cleaning (1000 Square Feet)	$100.00	$100.00	$100.00
Window Cleaning (10 Windows)	$90.00	$90.00	$90.00
Floor Treatments (100 Square Feet)	$11.00	$11.00	$11.00
Carpet Cleaning (100 Square Feet)	$80.00	$80.00	$80.00
Bathroom and Kitchen Cleaning (By Room)	$30.00	$30.00	$30.00
Sales			
Office Cleaning (1000 Square Feet)	$501,396	$800,000	$1,200,000
Window Cleaning (10	$72,595	$90,000	$112,500

Windows)			
Floor Treatments (100 Square Feet)	$10,899	$16,500	$22,000
Carpet Cleaning (100 Square Feet)	$104,325	$80,000	$100,000
Bathroom and Kitchen Cleaning (By Room)	$15,839	$15,000	$18,000
Total Sales	$705,053	$1,001,500	$1,452,500
Direct Unit Costs	Year 1	Year 2	Year 3
Office Cleaning (1000 Square Feet)	$35.00	$35.00	$35.00
Window Cleaning (10 Windows)	$36.00	$36.00	$36.00
Floor Treatments (100 Square Feet)	$4.40	$4.40	$4.40

Carpet Cleaning (100 Square Feet)		$32.00	$32.00	$32.00
Bathroom and Kitchen Cleaning (By Room)		$12.00	$12.00	$12.00
Direct Cost of Sales				
Office Cleaning (1000 Square Feet)	8	$175,488	$280,000	$420,000
Window Cleaning (10 Windows)		$29,038	$36,000	$45,000
Floor Treatments (100 Square Feet)		$4,360	$6,600	$8,800
Carpet Cleaning (100 Square Feet)		$41,730	$32,000	$40,000
Bathroom and Kitchen Cleaning (By Room)		$6,335	$6,000	$7,200

| Subtotal Direct Cost of Sales | 1 | $256,951 | $360,600 | $521,000 |

Chart: Sales Monthly

Chart: Sales by Year

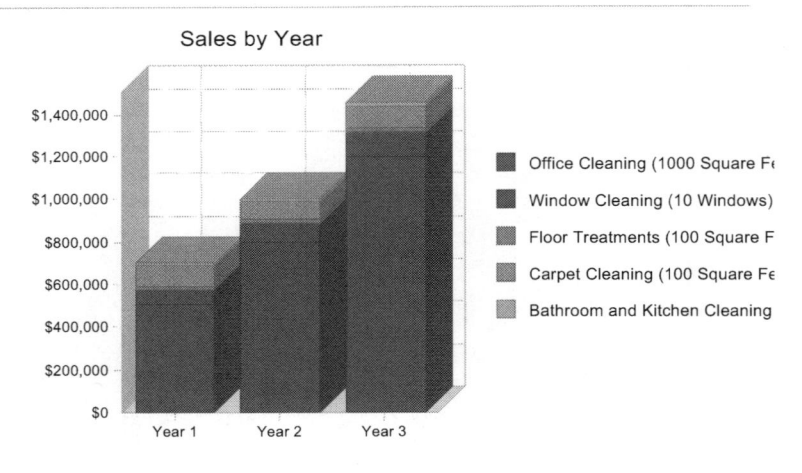

5.4 Milestones

Maria will head the sales activities, including prospecting and networking, to generate leads.

Jane Doe will manage the marketing and promotional activities including two trade shows (in January and February), the TV ad production (through a video production vendor), initial search engine optimization (through an SEO vendor), and the coupon campaign, which will cover three months of basic office cleaning for small-office clients.

Table: Milestones

Milestone	Start Date	End Date	Budget
Phone prospecting	11/1/2009	4/1/2010	$0
Business networking	11/1/2009	4/1/2010	$5,000
Entrepreneurship Trade Show	1/7/2010	1/9/2010	$10,000
Office Services Trade Show	2/9/2009	2/11/2009	$8,000
Coupon Campaign For Free Trial	11/1/2009	5/1/2009	$25,000
Initial Search Engine Optimization	11/1/2009	2/1/2010	$10,000
TV ad production	10/1/2009	11/15/2009	$20,000
Name me	9/1/2010	10/1/2010	$0

Name me	9/1/2010	10/1/2010	$0
Name me	9/1/2010	10/1/2010	$0
Totals			$78,000

Chart: Milestones

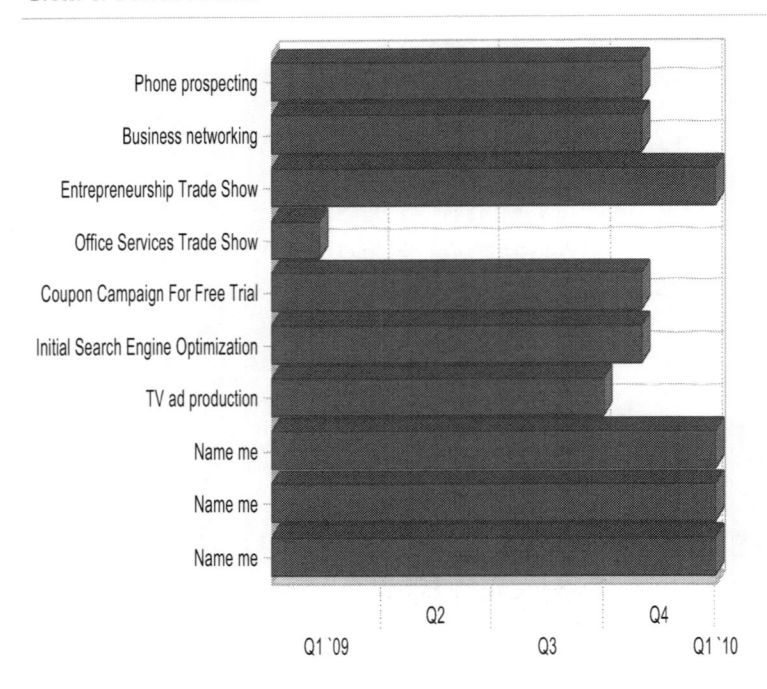

[Bar chart showing milestones across Q1 '09 through Q1 '10, with categories: Phone prospecting, Business networking, Entrepreneurship Trade Show, Office Services Trade Show, Coupon Campaign For Free Trial, Initial Search Engine Optimization, TV ad production, Name me, Name me, Name me]

6.0 Management Summary

Jane Doe and Maria Carmen will be the initial managers of the company. Jane Doe has ten years of experience as the store manager of a cleaning supply store, where she managed a staff of ten and was responsible for marketing, operations, and human resources. She will continue to manage those departments at Green Cleaning Services, and his title will be CEO.

Maria Carmen will manage sales and be the lead salesperson for the early operations of the firm. He has ten years of experience as an account executive for Clean-Pro, a commercial cleaning business. Maria's title will be Chief of Sales.

Financial management will be through a part-time accountant during the early operations of the firm.

6.1 Personnel Plan

The business will begin with minimal salaried staff, with most work performed by the two founders. The founders will be compensated through reasonable base salaries and will receive compensation through dividends and the growth of the business.

In the first year, an accountant will serve the role of Chief Financial Officer (CFO). In the second year, this will become a part-time position which will grow into a full-time position in the third year.

The operations assistant will be a basic administrative assistant focusing on the fulfillment of cleaning services, scheduling, quality assurance procedures, and human resources needs.

Total staff full-time equivalent on this chart include cleaning crew who work on an hourly basis and have their payroll assigned as costs of sales. One Cleaning Crew Head will be hired at the outset of the company, an additional Crew Head will be hired in the second year and a third in the third year.

Each will oversee crews of one to four members, and can also supplement their supervision responsibilities as members of crews under other supervisors. Cleaning crew members will grow from five in number at the outset of the business to 11 on average in the second year and 16 on average in the third year. All of these hourly staff will be hired when at least 20 hours per week of work is available, but their overtime will be limited. The business will hire additional employees rather than use significant overtime.

The cleaning crew will receive healthy base salaries as well as quarterly bonuses based on performance ratings from both their supervising cleaning crew head and clients. Crew heads will receive performance ratings from the company managers and clients to determine their quarterly bonuses.

Once the company reaches a sustainable level of profitability, the owners want to offer a health benefits plan for its employees, but this is not included within the plan's estimated expenses at this time.

Table: Personnel

Personnel Plan			
	Year 1	Year 2	Year 3
CEO	$48,000	$50,000	$52,000
Chief of Sales	$48,000	$50,000	$52,000
Accountant	$24,000	$40,000	$80,000
Operations Assistant	$36,000	$40,000	$45,000
Total People	13	16	24
Total Payroll	$156,000	$180,000	$229,000

7.0 Financial Plan

Green Cleaning Services will grow significantly, even over the first three years of operation, by taking advantage of the opportunity presented by its first target market, small offices, and leveraging its success there with medium and large offices. Growth of about $300,000 is expected in sales from the first year to second and over $400,000 from the second year to third.

Financing for this growth will come from the free cash flows generated by the healthy margins in this business once break-even volume has been achieved in the first year.

By the fifth year of operation, the business will be well-positioned for a strategic sale to a commercial cleaning franchise (one of the competitors discussed earlier) interested in expanding its expertise with small businesses. At this point, an exit will be possible for investors and the original owners.

1 Start-up Funding

Start-up funding will come in part from the financing of the initial purchases (delivery van, computer and cleaning equipment), and from credit card debt.

Beyond this debt financing, most start-up funding will be provided by the two founders and ;from additional angel investors. Once the additional investment has been contributed, the angel investors will own 49% of the business, Jane

Doe will own 26%, and Maria Carmen will own 25%.

Table: Start-up Funding

Start-up Funding	
Start-up Expenses to Fund	$33,500
Start-up Assets to Fund	$105,000
Total Funding Required	$138,500
Assets	
Non-cash Assets from Start-up	$45,000
Cash Requirements from Start-up	$60,000
Additional Cash Raised	$0
Cash Balance on Starting Date	$60,000
Total Assets	$105,000
Liabilities and Capital	
Liabilities	
Current Borrowing	$5,000
Long-term Liabilities	$20,000
Accounts Payable (Outstanding Bills)	$2,000
Other Current Liabilities (interest-free)	$0
Total Liabilities	$27,000
Maria Carmen	$25,000
Jane Doe	$25,000
Additional Investors	$61,500
Additional Investment Requirement	$0
Total Planned Investment	$111,500
Loss at Start-up (Start-up Expenses)	($33,500)
Total Capital	$78,000

Total Capital and Liabilities	$105,000
Total Funding	$138,500

7.2 Break-even Analysis

Each cleaning service offered has a healthy margin, and breakeven will occur around 552 units sold per month. This represents 512,000 square feet of offices or around 600 small business clients (or 400 small business and 100 medium business clients).

At this point, work will be both overnight and on weekends, with an average of 16 clients cleaned per day by shift workers. Six crews will be needed to provide this amount of service.

Table: Break-even Analysis

Break-even Analysis	
Monthly Units Break-even	552
Monthly Revenue Break-even	$45,012
Assumptions:	
Average Per-Unit Revenue	$81.58
Average Per-Unit Variable Cost	$29.73
Estimated Monthly Fixed Cost	$28,608

Chart: Break-even Analysis

Break-even Analysis

[Chart: Break-even Analysis, x-axis 0 to 1100, y-axis from ($25,000) to $30,000]

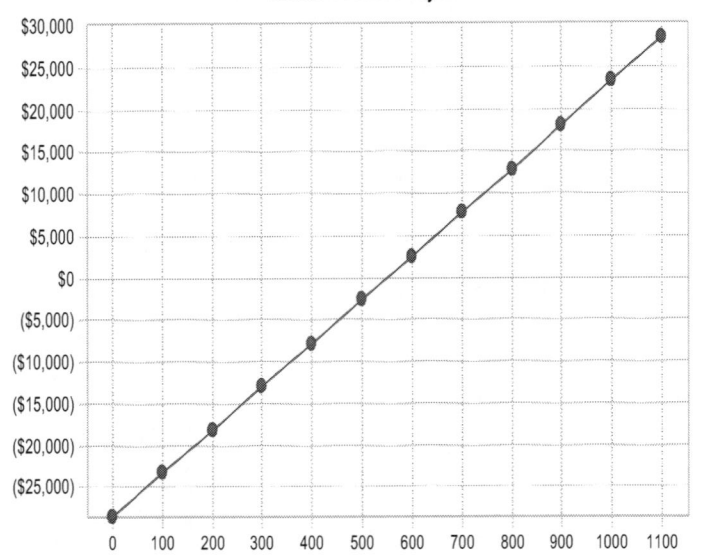

7.3 Projected Profit and Loss

Gross margins will remain relatively stable and grow slightly as better margin business (medium and large offices) is sought out, and better prices are established with vendors for volume discounts. The first year will represent a net profit of $71,000, which will continue to grow.

Table: Profit and Loss

Pro Forma Profit and Loss	Year 1	Year 2
Sales	$705,053	$1,001,500
Direct Cost of Sales	$256,951	$360,600
Other Costs of Sales	$0	$0
Total Cost of Sales	$256,951	$360,600

Gross Margin	$448,102	$640,900
Gross Margin %	63.56%	63.99%
Expenses		
Payroll	$156,000	$180,000
Marketing/Promotion	$79,000	$90,000
Depreciation	$18,400	$30,000
Rent	$30,000	$35,000
Utilities	$1,800	$2,400
Insurance	$3,000	$4,000
Payroll Taxes	$49,095	$63,060
Other	$6,000	$10,000
Total Operating Expenses	$343,295	$414,460
Profit Before Interest and Taxes	$104,807	$226,440
EBITDA	$123,207	$256,440
Interest Expense	$2,766	$4,809
Taxes Incurred	$30,612	$66,489
Net Profit	$71,429	$155,142
Net Profit/Sales	10.13%	15.49%

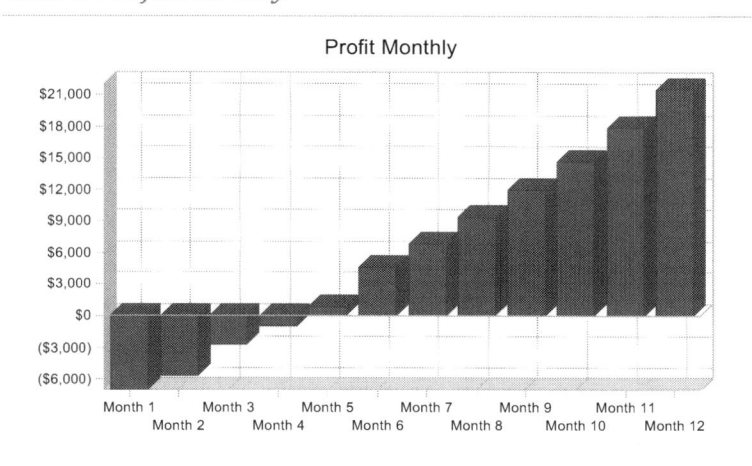

Chart: Profit Monthly

Chart: Profit Yearly

Profit Yearly

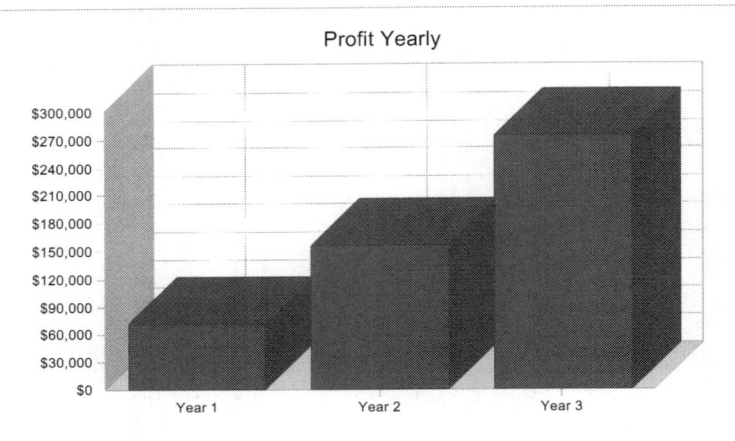

Chart: Gross Margin Monthly

Gross Margin Monthly

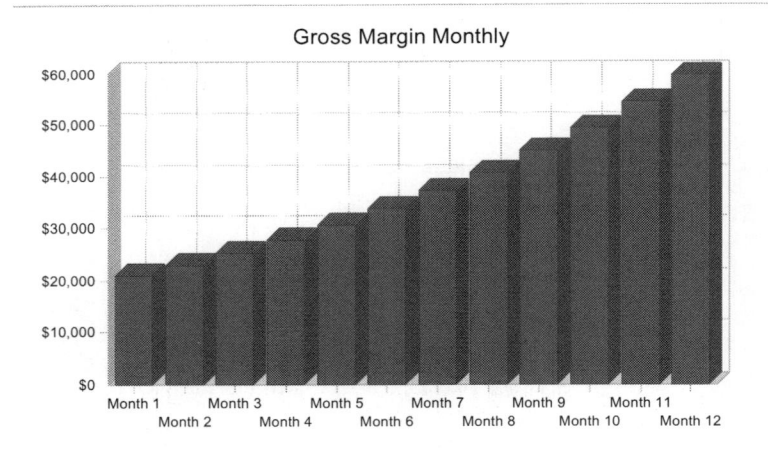

Chart: Gross Margin Yearly

Gross Margin Yearly

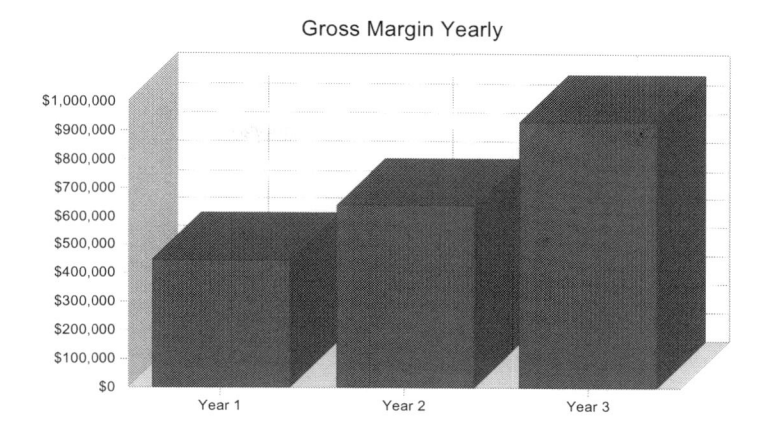

[Bar chart showing Gross Margin increasing from Year 1 to Year 3, with y-axis from $0 to $1,000,000]

7.4 Projected Cash Flow

Cash flow before dividends will be positive in the first year. Five months of negative cash flow are required for marketing activities to take hold before they show a greater effect on sales. Dividends can be paid out beginning in month nine to investors.

Accounts receivable will be collected in 30 days, but 45 days average has been given to be conservative.

The investment will be continually made for additional cleaning equipment and delivery vans to enable more cleaning crew to work. Furthermore, by the end of the first year, the office will expand to allow for additional storage and staff.

Table: Cash Flow

Pro Forma Cash Flow		
	Year 1	Year 2
Cash Received		

Cash from Operations		
Cash Sales	$0	$0
Cash from Receivables	$571,061	$945,162
Subtotal Cash from Operations	$571,061	$945,162
Additional Cash Received		
Sales Tax, VAT, HST/GST Received	$56,404	$80,120
New Current Borrowing	$10,000	$17,000
New Other Liabilities (interest-free)	$0	$0
New Long-term Liabilities	$20,000	$20,000
Sales of Other Current Assets	$0	$0
Sales of Long-term Assets	$0	$0
New Investment Received	$0	$0
Subtotal Cash Received	$657,465	$1,062,282
Expenditures	Year 1	Year 2
Expenditures from Operations		
Cash Spending	$156,000	$180,000
Bill Payments	$405,528	$639,751
Subtotal Spent on Operations	$561,528	$819,751
Additional Cash Spent		
Sales Tax, VAT, HST/GST Paid Out	$56,404	$80,120
Principal Repayment of Current	$7,913	$15,000

Borrowing Other Liabilities	$0	$0
Principal Repayment Long-term Liabilities	$6,000	$8,000
Principal Repayment Purchase Other Current Assets	$2,000	$15,000
Purchase Long-term Assets	$20,000	$20,000
Dividends	$20,000	$75,000
Subtotal Cash Spent	$673,845	$1,032,871
Net Cash Flow	($16,380)	$29,411
Cash Balance	$43,620	$73,031

Chart: Cash

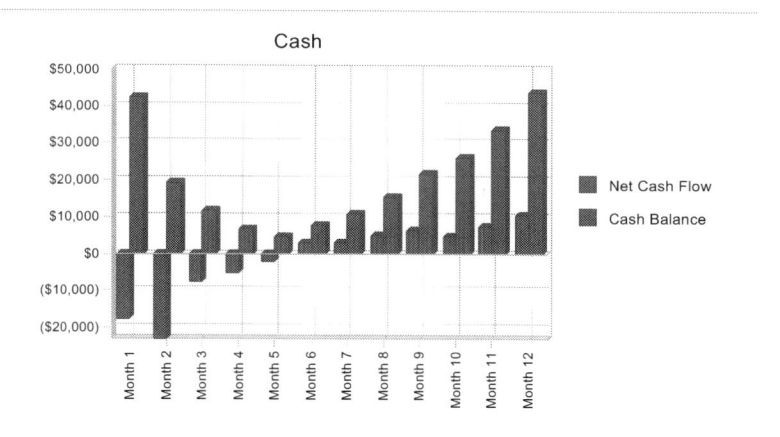

7.5 Projected Balance Sheet

The net worth of the business will grow significantly over the first three years of operation as the business will be primarily financed by its own earnings and not need to take on a great deal of new debt. The debt that is taken on will be financing for the purchases of new cleaning equipment and delivery vans, primarily.

Additional capital is not required over the first three years of operation as the free cash flows from the business will support the business.

Table: Balance Sheet

Pro Forma Balance Sheet		
	Year 1	Year 2
Assets		
Current Assets		
Cash	$43,620	$73,031
Accounts Receivable	$133,992	$190,330
Other Current Assets	$7,000	$22,000
Total Current Assets	$184,612	$285,361
Long-term Assets		
Long-term Assets	$60,000	$80,000
Accumulated Depreciation	$18,400	$48,400
Total Long-term Assets	$41,600	$31,600
Total Assets	$226,212	$316,961
Liabilities and Capital	Year 1	Year 2
Current Liabilities		
Accounts Payable	$55,696	$52,303
Current Borrowing	$7,087	$9,087
Other Current Liabilities	$0	$0
Subtotal Current Liabilities	$62,784	$61,391
Long-term Liabilities	$34,000	$46,000

Total Liabilities	$96,784	$107,391
Paid-in Capital	$111,500	$111,500
Retained Earnings	($53,500)	($57,071)
Earnings	$71,429	$155,142
Total Capital	$129,429	$209,570
Total Liabilities and Capital	$226,212	$316,961
Net Worth	$129,429	$209,570

7.6 Business Ratios

This table shows ratios for the three years of the plan compared to the janitorial services businesses of similar revenues. Green Cleaning Services expects to improve on industry profitability, as shown in this table, even with slightly higher spending on S G A and advertising as a percentage of sales. Gross margins will be slightly better than the comparable industry gross margins.

Table: Ratios

Ratio Analysis	Year 1	Year 2	Industry Profile
Sales Growth	n.a.	42.05%	0.77%
Percent of Total Assets			
Accounts Receivable	59.23%	60.05%	14.54%
Other Current Assets	3.09%	6.94%	37.68%
Total Current Assets	81.61%	90.03%	54.28%

Long-term Assets	18.39%	9.97%	45.72%
Total Assets	100.00%	100.00%	100.00%
Current Liabilities	27.75%	19.37%	28.46%
Long-term Liabilities	15.03%	14.51%	71.54%
Total Liabilities	42.78%	33.88%	100.00%
Net Worth	57.22%	66.12%	0.00%
Percent of Sales			
Sales	100.00%	100.00%	100.00%
Gross Margin	63.56%	63.99%	62.79%
Selling, General Expenses	53.42%	48.50%	17.10%
Advertising Expenses	11.20%	8.99%	0.21%
Profit Before Interest and Taxes	14.87%	22.61%	5.93%
Main Ratios			
Current	2.94	4.65	1.35
Quick	2.94	4.65	1.28
Total Debt to Total Assets	42.78%	33.88%	100.00%
Net Working Capital	$121,829	$223,970	n.a
Interest Coverage	37.90	47.09	n.a

Additional Ratios			
Assets to Sales	0.32	0.32	n.a
Current Debt/Total Assets	28%	19%	n.a
Acid Test	0.81	1.55	n.a
Sales/Net Worth	5.45	4.78	n.a
Dividend Payout	0.28	0.48	n.a

Employee Written Warning Letter

Employee:	
Employee ID:	_____
Employee Title:	Crew
Manager:	Maria Carmen
HR Officer:	_____
Date:	October 31, 2015

Introduction

1. Green Cleaning Services (the "Employer") recognizes the importance of maintaining a consistent and experienced workforce. As such, it is important to retain staff wherever possible. It is the desire of Green Cleaning Services to retain *employee name* (the "Employee"); however, some changes in work behavior must occur in order to ensure a successful working relationship.

Infraction

2. This Employee Warning Letter (the "Letter") concerns the Employee's failure to fulfill work obligations that occurred on or about October 31, 2015:

   - _____
     _____
     _____
     _____
     _____

_____
_____
_____
_____
_____
_____
_____

3. This is the first occurrence of this type of infraction.

Follow-up Assessment

4. A follow-up meeting is scheduled for November 30, 2015, to review the Employee's progress. A review meeting may also be called at any time prior to that date if there is a re-occurrence of any unacceptable behavior.

Consequences

5. Because of the effect of the Employee's behavior on critical customer relations, any re-occurrence of the unacceptable behavior may result in termination of employment for the Employee at the sole discretion of the company.

Employee Signature

6. By signing this form, the Employee is not making any admission of wrong-doing, nor is the Employee necessarily agreeing with the content of this Letter. The Employee's signature only acknowledges that the Employee has received this Letter.

Signature of Employee

_____

Signature of Manager

_____

Date

_____

Made in United States
Orlando, FL
27 May 2023